FOUR GREAT AMERICANS

FOUR GREAT AMERICANS

BY

JAMES BALDWIN

YESTERDAY'S CLASSICS

CHAPEL HILL, NORTH CAROLINA

Cover and arrangement © 2007 Yesterday's Classics, LLC.

This edition, first published in 2007 by Yesterday's Classics, an imprint of Yesterday's Classics, LLC, is an unabridged republication of the work originally published by Werner School Book Company in 1896. For the complete listing of the books that are published by Yesterday's Classics, please visit www.yesterdaysclassics.com. Yesterday's Classics is the publishing arm of the Baldwin Online Children's Literature Project which presents the complete text of hundreds of classic books for children at www.mainlesson.com.

ISBN-10: 1-59915-219-3

ISBN-13: 978-1-59915-219-6

Yesterday's Classics, LLC
PO Box 3418
Chapel Hill, NC 27515

CONTENTS

GEORGE WASHINGTON

WHEN WASHINGTON WAS A BOY	1
HIS HOMES	3
HIS SCHOOLS AND SCHOOLMASTERS	5
GOING TO SEA	8
THE YOUNG SURVEYOR	12
THE OHIO COUNTRY	17
A CHANGE OF CIRCUMSTANCES	20
A PERILOUS JOURNEY	21
HIS FIRST BATTLE	24
THE FRENCH AND INDIAN WAR	26
THE MUTTERINGS OF THE STORM	31
THE BEGINNING OF THE WAR	35
INDEPENDENCE	38
THE FIRST PRESIDENT	41
"FIRST IN WAR, FIRST IN PEACE"	44

BENJAMIN FRANKLIN

THE WHISTLE 49
SCHOOLDAYS 52
THE BOYS AND THE WHARF 54
CHOOSING A TRADE 55
HOW FRANKLIN EDUCATED HIMSELF 57
FAREWELL TO BOSTON 60
THE FIRST DAY IN PHILADELPHIA 63
GOVERNOR WILLIAM KEITH 66
THE RETURN TO PHILADELPHIA 69
THE FIRST VISIT TO ENGLAND 72
A LEADING MAN IN PHILADELPHIA 74
FRANKLIN'S RULES OF LIFE 76
FRANKLIN'S SERVICES TO THE COLONIES 78
FRANKLIN'S WONDERFUL KITE 82
THE LAST YEARS 86

DANIEL WEBSTER

CAPTAIN WEBSTER	93
THE YOUNGEST SON	96
EZEKIEL AND DANIEL	99
PLANS FOR THE FUTURE	101
AT EXETER ACADEMY	104
GETTING READY FOR COLLEGE	107
AT DARTMOUTH COLLEGE	110
HOW DANIEL TAUGHT SCHOOL	113
DANIEL GOES TO BOSTON	117
LAWYER AND CONGRESSMAN	121
THE DARTMOUTH COLLEGE CASE	125
WEBSTER'S GREAT ORATIONS	126
MR. WEBSTER IN THE SENATE	128
MR. WEBSTER IN PRIVATE LIFE	131
THE LAST YEARS	134

ABRAHAM LINCOLN

The Kentucky Home 141

Work and Sorrow... 145

The New Mother 150

School and Books.. 152

Life in the Backwoods 155

The Boatman 158

The First Years in Illinois........................... 160

The Black Hawk War 162

In the Legislature 164

Politics and Marriage 168

Congressman and Lawyer 170

The Question of Slavery 173

Lincoln and Douglas 177

President of the United States 180

The End of a Great Life 183

THE STORY OF GEORGE WASHINGTON

G Washington

GEORGE WASHINGTON

When Washington was a Boy

When George Washington was a boy there was no United States. The land was here, just as it is now, stretching from the Atlantic Ocean to the Pacific; but nearly all of it was wild and unknown.

Between the Atlantic Ocean and the Allegheny Mountains there were thirteen colonies, or great settlements. The most of the people who lived in these colonies were English people, or the children of English people; and so the King of England made their laws and appointed their governors.

The newest of the colonies was Georgia, which was settled the year after George Washington was born.

The oldest colony was Virginia, which had been settled one hundred and twenty-five years. It was also the richest colony, and more people were living in it than in any other.

There were only two or three towns in Virginia at that time, and they were quite small.

Most of the people lived on farms or on big plantations, where they raised whatever they needed to eat. They also raised tobacco, which they sent to England to be sold.

The farms, or plantations, were often far apart, with stretches of thick woods between them. Nearly every one was close to a river, or some other large body of water; for there are many rivers in Virginia.

There were no roads, such as we have nowadays, but only paths through the woods. When people wanted to travel from place to place, they had to go on foot, or on horseback, or in small boats.

A few of the rich men who lived on the big plantations had coaches; and now and then they would drive out in grand style behind four or six horses, with a fine array of servants and outriders following them. But they could not drive far where there were no roads, and we can hardly understand how they got any pleasure out of it.

Nearly all the work on the plantations was done by slaves. Ships had been bringing negroes from Africa for more than a hundred years, and now nearly half the people in Virginia were blacks.

Very often, also, poor white men from England were sold as slaves for a few years in order to pay for their passage across the ocean. When their freedom was given to them they continued to work at whatever they could find to do; or they cleared small farms in the woods for themselves, or went farther to the west and became woodsmen and hunters.

There was but very little money in Virginia at that time, and, indeed, there was not much use for it. For what could be done with money where there were no shops worth speaking of, and no stores, and nothing to buy?

The common people raised flax and wool, and wove their own cloth; and they made their own tools and furniture. The rich people did the same; but for their better or finer goods they sent to England.

For you must know that in all this country there were no great mills for spinning and weaving as there are now; there were no factories of any kind; there were no foundries where iron could be melted and shaped into all kinds of useful and beautiful things.

When George Washington was a boy the world was not much like it is now.

His Homes

George Washington's father owned a large plantation on the western shore of the Potomac River. George's great-grandfather, John Washington, had settled upon it nearly eighty years before, and there the family had dwelt ever since.

This plantation was in Westmoreland county, not quite forty miles above the place where the Potomac flows into Chesapeake Bay. By looking at your map of Virginia, you will see that the river is very broad there.

On one side of the plantation, and flowing through it, there was a creek, called Bridge's Creek; and for this reason the place was known as the Bridge's Creek Plantation.

It was here, on the 22d of February, 1732, that George Washington was born.

Although his father was a rich man, the house in which he lived was neither very large nor very fine—at least it would not be thought so now.

It was a square, wooden building, with four rooms on the ground floor and an attic above.

The eaves were low, and the roof was long and sloping. At each end of the house there was a huge chimney; and inside were big fireplaces, one for the kitchen and one for the "great room" where visitors were received.

But George did not live long in this house. When he was about three years old his father moved to another plantation which he owned, near Hunting Creek several miles farther up the river. This new plantation was at first known as the Washington Plantation, but it is now called Mount Vernon.

Four years after this the house of the Washingtons was burned down. But Mr. Washington had still other lands on the Rappahannock River. He had also an interest in some iron mines that were being opened there. And so to this place the family was now taken.

The house by the Rappahannock was very much like the one at Bridge's Creek. It stood on high ground, overlooking the river and some low meadows; and on the other side of the river was the village of Fredericksburg, which at that time was a very small village indeed.

George was now about seven years old.

His Schools and Schoolmasters

There were no good schools in Virginia at that time. In fact, the people did not care much about learning.

There were few educated men besides the parsons, and even some of the parsons were very ignorant.

It was the custom of some of the richest families to send their eldest sons to England to the great schools there. But it is doubtful if these young men learned much about books.

They spent a winter or two in the gay society of London, and were taught the manners of gentlemen— and that was about all.

George Washington's father, when a young man, had spent some time at Appleby School in England, and George's half-brothers, Lawrence and Augustine, who were several years older than he, had been sent to the same school.

But book-learning was not thought to be of much use. To know how to manage the business of a plantation, to be polite to one's equals, to be a leader in the affairs of the colony—this was thought to be the best education.

And so, for most of the young men, it was enough if they could read and write a little and keep a few simple accounts. As for the girls, the parson might give them a few lessons now and then; and if they learned good manners and could write letters to their friends, what more could they need?

George Washington's first teacher was a poor sexton, whose name was Mr. Hobby. There is a story that he had been too poor to pay his passage from England, and that he had, therefore, been sold to Mr. Washington as a slave for a short time; but how true this is, I cannot say.

From Mr. Hobby, George learned to spell easy words, and perhaps to write a little; but, although he afterward became a very careful and good penman, he was a poor speller as long as he lived.

When George was about eleven years old his father died. We do not know what his father's intentions had been regarding him. But possibly, if he had lived, he would have given George the best education that his means would afford.

But now everything was changed. The plantation at Hunting Creek, and, indeed almost all the rest of Mr. Washington's great estate, became the property of the eldest son, Lawrence.

George was sent to Bridge's Creek to live for a while with his brother Augustine, who now owned the old home plantation there. The mother and the younger children remained on the Rappahannock farm.

While at Bridge's Creek, George was sent to school to a Mr. Williams, who had lately come from England.

There are still to be seen some exercises which the lad wrote at that time. There is also a little book, called *The Young Man's Companion*, from which he copied, with great care, a set of rules for good behavior and right living.

Not many boys twelve years old would care for such a book nowadays. But you must know that in those days there were no books for children, and, indeed, very few for older people.

The maxims and wise sayings which George copied were, no doubt, very interesting to him—so interesting that many of them were never forgotten.

There are many other things also in this *Young Man's Companion*, and we have reason to believe that George studied them all.

There are short chapters on arithmetic and surveying, rules for the measuring of land and lumber, and a set of forms for notes, deeds, and other legal documents. A knowledge of these things was, doubtless, of greater importance to him than the reading of many books would have been.

Just what else George may have studied in Mr. William's school I cannot say. But all this time he was growing to be a stout, manly boy, tall and strong, and well-behaved. And both his brothers and himself were beginning to think of what he should do when he should become a man.

Going to Sea

Once every summer a ship came up the river to the plantation, and was moored near the shore.

It had come across the sea from far-away England, and it brought many things for those who were rich enough to pay for them.

It brought bonnets and pretty dresses for George's mother and sisters; it brought perhaps a hat and a tailor-made suit for himself; it brought tools and furniture, and once a yellow coach that had been made in London, for his brother.

When all these things had been taken ashore, the ship would hoist her sails and go on, farther up the river, to leave goods at other plantations.

In a few weeks it would come back and be moored again at the same place.

Then there was a busy time on shore. The tobacco that had been raised during the last year must be carried on shipboard to be taken to the great tobacco markets in England.

The slaves on the plantation were running back and forth, rolling barrels and carrying bales of tobacco down to the landing.

Letters were written to friends in England, and orders were made out for the goods that were to be brought back next year.

But in a day or two, all this stir was over. The sails were again spread, and the ship glided away on its long voyage across the sea.

George had seen this ship coming and going every year since he could remember. He must have thought how pleasant it would be to sail away to foreign lands and see the many wonderful things that are there.

And then, like many another active boy, he began to grow tired of the quiet life on the farm, and wish that he might be a sailor.

He was now about fourteen years old. Since the death of his father, his mother had found it hard work, with her five children, to manage her farm on the Rappahannock and make everything come out even at the end of each year. Was it not time that George should be earning something for himself? But what should he do?

He wanted to go to sea. His brother Lawrence, and even his mother, thought that this might be the best thing.

A bright boy like George would not long be a common sailor. He would soon make his way to a high place in the king's navy. So, at least, his friends believed.

And so the matter was at last settled. A sea-captain who was known to the family, agreed to take George with him. He was to sail in a short time.

The day came. His mother, his brothers, his sisters, were all there to bid him good-bye. But in the meanwhile a letter had come to his mother, from his uncle who lived in England.

"If you care for the boy's future," said the letter, "do not let him go to sea. Places in the king's navy are not easy to obtain. If he begins as a sailor, he will never be aught else."

The letter convinced George's mother—it half convinced his brothers—that this going to sea would be a sad mistake. But George, like other boys of his age, was headstrong. He would not listen to reason. A sailor he would be.

The ship was in the river waiting for him. A boat had come to the landing to take him on board.

The little chest which held his clothing had been carried down to the bank. George was in high glee at the thought of going.

"Good-bye, mother," he said.

GEORGE WASHINGTON

He stood on the doorstep and looked back into the house. He saw the kind faces of those whom he loved. He began to feel very sad at the thought of leaving them.

"Good-bye, George!"

He saw the tears welling up in his mother's eyes. He saw them rolling down her cheeks. He knew now that she did not want him to go. He could not bear to see her grief.

"Mother, I have changed my mind," he said. "I will not be a sailor. I will not leave you."

Then he turned to the black boy who was waiting by the door, and said, "Run down to the landing and tell them not to put the chest on board. Tell them that I have thought differently of the matter and that I am going to stay at home."

If George had not changed his mind, but had really gone to sea, how different the history of this country would have been!

He now went to his studies with a better will than before; and although he read but few books he learned much that was useful to him in life. He studied surveying with especial care, and made himself as thorough in that branch of knowledge as it was possible to do with so few advantages.

The Young Surveyor

Lawrence Washington was about fourteen years older than his brother George.

As I have already said, he had been to England and had spent some time at Appleby School. He had served in the king's army for a little while, and had been with Admiral Vernon's squadron in the West Indies.

He had formed so great a liking for the admiral that when he came home he changed the name of his plantation at Hunting Creek, and called it Mount Vernon—a name by which it is still known.

Not far from Mount Vernon there was another fine plantation called Belvoir, that was owned by William Fairfax, an English gentleman of much wealth and influence. Now this Mr. Fairfax had a young daughter, as wise as she was beautiful; and so, what should Lawrence Washington do but ask her to be his wife? He built a large house at Mount Vernon with a great porch fronting on the Potomac; and when Miss Fairfax became Mrs. Washington and went into this home as its mistress, people said that there was not a handsomer or happier young couple in all Virginia.

After young George Washington had changed his mind about going to sea, he went up to Mount Vernon to live with his elder brother. For Lawrence had great love for the boy, and treated him as his father would have done.

GEORGE WASHINGTON

At Mount Vernon George kept on with his studies in surveying. He had a compass and surveyor's chain, and hardly a day passed that he was not out on the plantation, running lines and measuring his brother's fields.

Sometimes when he was busy at this kind of work, a tall, white-haired gentleman would come over from Belvoir to see what he was doing and to talk with him. This gentleman was Sir Thomas Fairfax, a cousin of the owner of Belvoir. He was sixty years old, and had lately come from England to look after his lands in Virginia; for he was the owner of many thousands of acres among the mountains and in the wild woods.

Sir Thomas was a courtly old gentleman, and he had seen much of the world. He was a fine scholar; and had been a soldier, and then a man of letters; and he belonged to a rich and noble family.

It was not long until he and George were the best of friends. Often they would spend the morning together, talking or surveying; and in the afternoon they would ride out with servants and hounds, hunting foxes and making fine sport of it among the woods and hills.

And when Sir Thomas Fairfax saw how manly and brave his young friend was, and how very exact and careful in all that he did, he said: "Here is a boy who gives promise of great things. I can trust him."

Before the winter was over he had made a bargain with George to survey his lands that lay beyond the Blue Ridge Mountains.

I have already told you that at this time nearly all the country west of the mountains was a wild and unknown region. In fact, all the western part of Virginia was an unbroken wilderness, with only here and there a hunter's camp or the solitary hut of some daring woodsman.

But Sir Thomas hoped that by having the land surveyed, and some part of it laid out into farms, people might be persuaded to go there and settle. And who in all the colony could do this work better than his young friend, George Washington?

It was a bright day in March, 1748, when George started out on his first trip across the mountains. His only company was a young son of William Fairfax of Belvoir.

The two friends were mounted on good horses; and both had guns, for there was fine hunting in the woods. It was nearly a hundred miles to the mountain-gap through which they passed into the country beyond. As there were no roads, but only paths through the forest, they could not travel very fast.

After several days they reached the beautiful valley of the Shenandoah. They now began their surveying. They went up the river for some distance; then they crossed and went down on the other side. At last they reached the Potomac River, near where Harpers Ferry now stands.

At night they slept sometimes by a camp fire in the woods, and sometimes in the rude hut of a settler or a hunter. They were often wet and cold. They cooked their meat by broiling it on sticks above the coals. They ate without dishes, and drank water from the running streams.

One day they met a party of Indians, the first red men they had seen. There were thirty of them, with their bodies painted in true savage style; for they were just going home from a war with some other tribe.

The Indians were very friendly to the young surveyors. It was evening, and they built a huge fire under the trees. Then they danced their war dance around it, and sang and yelled and made hideous sport until far in the night.

To George and his friend it was a strange sight; but they were brave young men, and not likely to be afraid even though the danger had been greater.

They had many other adventures in the woods of which I cannot tell you in this little book—shooting wild game, swimming rivers, climbing mountains. But about the middle of April they returned in safety to Mount Vernon.

It would seem that the object of this first trip was to get a general knowledge of the extent of Sir Thomas Fairfax's great woodland estate—to learn where the richest bottom lands lay, and where were the best hunting grounds.

The young men had not done much if any real surveying; they had been exploring.

George Washington had written an account of everything in a little notebook which he carried with him.

Sir Thomas was so highly pleased with the report which the young men brought back that he made up his mind to move across the Blue Ridge and spend the rest of his life on his own lands.

And so, that very summer, he built in the midst of the great woods a hunting lodge which he called Greenway Court. It was a large, square house, with broad gables and a long roof sloping almost to the ground.

When he moved into this lodge he expected soon to build a splendid mansion and make a grand home there, like the homes he had known in England. But time passed, and as the lodge was roomy and comfortable, he still lived in it and put off beginning another house.

Washington was now seventeen years old. Through the influence of Sir Thomas Fairfax he was appointed public surveyor; and nothing would do but that he must spend the most of his time at Greenway Court and keep on with the work that he had begun.

For the greater part of three years he worked in the woods and among the mountains, surveying Sir Thomas's lands. And Sir Thomas paid him well—a doubloon ($8.24) for each day, and more than that if the work was very hard.

But there were times when the young surveyor did not go out to work, but stayed at Greenway Court with his good friend, Sir Thomas. The old gentleman had something of a library, and on days when they could neither work nor hunt, George spent the time in

GEORGE WASHINGTON

reading. He read the *Spectator* and a history of England, and possibly some other works.

And so it came about that the three years which young Washington spent in surveying were of much profit to him.

The work in the open air gave him health and strength. He gained courage and self-reliance. He became acquainted with the ways of the backwoodsmen and of the savage Indians. And from Sir Thomas Fairfax he learned a great deal about the history, the laws, and the military affairs of old England.

And in whatever he undertook to do or to learn, he was careful and systematic and thorough. He did nothing by guess; he never left anything half done. And therein, let me say to you, lie the secrets of success in any calling.

The Ohio Country

You have already learned how the English people had control of all that part of our country which borders upon the Atlantic Ocean. You have learned, also, that they had made thirteen great settlements along the coast, while all the vast region west of the mountains remained a wild and unknown land.

Now, because Englishmen had been the first white men to see the line of shore that stretches from Maine to Georgia, they set up a claim to all the land west of that line.

They had no idea how far the land extended. They knew almost nothing about its great rivers, its vast forests, its lofty mountains, its rich prairies. They cared nothing for the claims of the Indians whose homes were there.

"All the land from ocean to ocean," they said, "belongs to the King of England."

But there were other people who also had something to say about this matter.

The French had explored the Mississippi River. They had sailed on the Great Lakes. Their hunters and trappers were roaming through the western forests. They had made treaties with the Indians; and they had built trading posts, here and there, along the watercourses.

They said, "The English people may keep their strip of land between the mountains and the sea. But these great river valleys and this country around the Lakes are ours, because we have been the first to explore and make use of them."

Now, about the time that George Washington was thinking of becoming a sailor, some of the rich planters in Virginia began to hear wonderful stories about a fertile region west of the Alleghenies, watered by a noble river, and rich in game and fur-bearing animals.

This region was called the Ohio Country, from the name of the river; and those who took pains to learn the most about it were satisfied that it would, at some time, be of very great importance to the people who should control it.

And so these Virginian planters and certain Englishmen formed a company called the Ohio Company, the object of which was to explore the country, and make money by establishing trading posts and settlements there. And of this company, Lawrence Washington was one of the chief managers.

Lawrence Washington and his brother George had often talked about this enterprise.

"We shall have trouble with the French," said Lawrence. "They have already sent men into the Ohio Country; and they are trying in every way to prove that the land belongs to them."

"It looks as if we should have to drive them out by force," said George.

"Yes, and there will probably be some hard fighting," said Lawrence; "and you, as a young man, must get yourself ready to have a hand in it."

And Lawrence followed this up by persuading the governor of the colony to appoint George as one of the adjutants-general of Virginia.

George was only nineteen years old, but he was now Major Washington, and one of the most promising soldiers in America.

A Change of Circumstances

Although George Washington spent so much of his time at Greenway Court, he still called Mount Vernon his home.

Going down home in the autumn, just before he was twenty years old, he found matters in a sad state, and greatly changed.

His brother Lawrence was very ill—indeed, he had been ill a long time. He had tried a trip to England; he had spent a summer at the warm springs; but all to no purpose. He was losing strength every day.

The sick man dreaded the coming of cold weather. If he could only go to the warm West Indies before winter set in, perhaps that would prolong his life. Would George go with him?

No loving brother could refuse a request like that.

The captain of a ship in the West India trade agreed to take them; and so, while it was still pleasant September, the two Washingtons embarked for Barbadoes, which, then as now, belonged to the English.

It was the first time that George had ever been outside of his native land, and it proved to be also the last. He took careful notice of everything that he saw; and, in the little notebook which he seems to have always had with him, he wrote a brief account of the trip.

He had not been three weeks at Barbadoes before he was taken down with the smallpox; and for a month he was very sick. And so his winter in the West Indies could not have been very pleasant.

In February the two brothers returned home to Mount Vernon. Lawrence's health had not been bettered by the journey. He was now very feeble; but he lingered on until July, when he died.

By his will Lawrence Washington left his fine estate of Mount Vernon, and all the rest of his wealth, to his little daughter. But George was to be the daughter's guardian; and in case of her death, all her vast property was to be his own.

And so, before he was quite twenty-one years old, George Washington was settled at Mount Vernon as the manager of one of the richest estates in Virginia. The death of his little niece not long afterward made him the owner of this estate, and, of course, a very wealthy man.

But within a brief time, events occurred which called him way from his peaceful employments.

A Perilous Journey

Early the very next year news was brought to Virginia that the French were building forts along the

Ohio, and making friends with the Indians there. This of course meant that they intended to keep the English out of that country.

The governor of Virginia thought that the time had come to speak out about this matter. He would send a messenger with a letter to these Frenchmen, telling them that all the land belonged to the English, and that no trespassing would be allowed.

The first messenger that he sent became alarmed before he was within a hundred miles of a Frenchman, and went back to say that everything was as good as lost.

It was very plain that a man with some courage must be chosen for such an undertaking.

"I will send Major George Washington," said the governor. "He is very young, but he is the bravest man in the colony."

Now, promptness was one of those traits of character which made George Washington the great man which he afterward became. And so, on the very day that he received his appointment he set out for the Ohio Country.

He took with him three white hunters, two Indians, and a famous woodsman, whose name was Christopher Gist. A small tent or two, and such few things as they would need on the journey, were strapped on the backs of horses.

They pushed through the woods in a northwestwardly direction, and at last reached a place called Venango, not very far from where Pittsburgh now stands. This was the first outpost of the French; and there Washington met some of the French officers, and heard them talk about what they proposed to do.

Then, after a long ride to the north, they came to another fort. The French commandant was here, and he welcomed Washington with a great show of kindness.

Washington gave him the letter which he had brought from the governor of Virginia.

The commandant read it, and two days afterward gave him an answer.

He said that he would forward the letter to the French governor; but as for the Ohio Country, he had been ordered to hold it, and he meant to do so.

Of course Washington could do nothing further. But it was plain to him that the news ought to be carried back to Virginia without delay.

It was now midwinter. As no horse could travel through the trackless woods at this time of year, he must make his way on foot.

So, with only the woodsman, Gist, he shouldered his rifle and knapsack, and bravely started home.

It was a terrible journey. The ground was covered with snow; the rivers were frozen; there was not even a path through the forest. If Gist had not been so fine a woodsman they would hardly have seen Virginia again.

Once an Indian shot at Washington from behind a tree. Once the brave young man fell into a river, among floating ice, and would have been drowned but for Gist.

At last they reached the house of a trader on the Monongahela River. There they were kindly welcomed, and urged to stay until the weather should grow milder.

But Washington would not delay.

Sixteen days after that, he was back in Virginia, telling the governor all about his adventures, and giving his opinion about the best way to deal with the French.

His First Battle

It was now very plain that if the English were going to hold the Ohio Country and the vast western region which they claimed as their own, they must fight for it.

The people of Virginia were not very anxious to go to war. But their governor was not willing to be beaten by the French.

He made George Washington a lieutenant-colonel of Virginia troops and set about raising an army to send into the Ohio country.

Early in the spring Colonel Washington, with a hundred and fifty men, was marching across the country toward the head waters of the Ohio. It was a small

GEORGE WASHINGTON

army to advance against the thousands of French and Indians who now held that region.

But other officers, with stronger forces, were expected to follow close behind.

Late in May the little army reached the valley of the Monongahela, and began to build a fort at a place called Great Meadows.

By this time the French and Indians were aroused, and hundreds of them were hurrying forward to defend the Ohio Country from the English. One of their scouting parties, coming up the river, was met by Washington with forty men.

The French were not expecting any foe at this place. There were but thirty-two of them; and of these only one escaped. Ten were killed, and the rest were taken prisoners.

This was Washington's first battle, and he was more proud of it than you might suppose. He sent his prisoners to Virginia, and was ready now, with his handful of men, to meet all the French and Indians that might come against him!

And they did come, and in greater numbers than he had expected. He made haste to finish, if possible, the fort that had been begun.

But they were upon him before he was ready. They had four men to his one. They surrounded the fort and shut his little Virginian army in.

What could Colonel Washington do? His soldiers were already half-starved. There was but little food in the fort, and no way to get any more.

The French leader asked if he did not think it would be a wise thing to surrender. Washington hated the very thought of it; but nothing else could be done.

"If you will march your men straight home and give me a pledge that they and all Virginians will stay out of the Ohio Country for the next twelve months, you may go," said the Frenchman.

It was done.

Washington, full of disappointment, went back to Mount Vernon. But he felt more like fighting than ever before.

He was now twenty-two years old.

The French and Indian War

In the meanwhile the King of England had heard how the French were building forts along the Ohio and how they were sending their traders to the Great Lakes and to the valley of the Mississippi.

"If we allow them to go on in this way, they will soon take all that vast western country away from us," he said.

And so, the very next winter, he sent over an army under General Edward Braddock to drive the French out of that part of America and at the same time teach their Indian friends a lesson.

It was in February, 1755, when General Braddock and his troops went into camp at Alexandria in

Virginia. As Alexandria was only a few miles from Mount Vernon, Washington rode over to see the fine array and become acquainted with the officers.

When General Braddock heard that this was the young man who had ventured so boldly into the Ohio Country, he offered him a place on his staff. This was very pleasing to Washington, for there was nothing more attractive to him than soldiering.

It was several weeks before the army was ready to start: and then it moved so slowly that it did not reach the Monongahela until July.

The soldiers in their fine uniforms made a splendid appearance as they marched in regular order across the country.

Benjamin Franklin, one of the wisest men in America, had told General Braddock that his greatest danger would be from unseen foes hidden among the underbrush and trees.

"They may be dangerous to your backwoodsmen," said Braddock; "but to the trained soldiers of the king they can give no trouble at all."

But scarcely had the army crossed the Monongahela when it was fired upon by unseen enemies. The woods rang with the cries of savage men.

The soldiers knew not how to return the fire. They were shot down in their tracks like animals in a pen.

"Let the men take to the shelter of the trees!" was Washington's advice.

But Braddock would not listen to it. They must keep in order and fight as they had been trained to fight.

Washington rode hither and thither trying his best to save the day. Two horses were shot under him; four bullets passed through his coat; and still he was unhurt. The Indians thought that he bore a charmed life, for none of them could hit him.

It was a dreadful affair—more like a slaughter than a battle. Seven hundred of Braddock's fine soldiers, and more than half of his officers, were killed or wounded. And all this havoc was made by two hundred Frenchmen and about six hundred Indians hidden among the trees.

At last Braddock gave the order to retreat. It soon became a wild flight rather than a retreat; and yet, had it not been for Washington, it would have been much worse.

The General himself had been fatally wounded. There was no one but Washington who could restore courage to the frightened men, and lead them safely from the place of defeat.

Four days after the battle General Braddock died, and the remnant of the army being now led by a Colonel Dunbar, hurried back to the eastern settlements.

Of all the men who took part in that unfortunate expedition against the French, there was only one who gained any renown therefrom, and that one was Colonel George Washington.

GEORGE WASHINGTON

He went back to Mount Vernon, wishing never to be sent to the Ohio Country again.

The people of Virginia were so fearful lest the French and Indians should follow up their victory and attack the settlements, that they quickly raised a regiment of a thousand men to defend their colony. And so highly did they esteem Colonel Washington that they made him commander of all the forces of the colony, to do with them as he might deem best.

The war with the French for the possession of the Ohio Country and the valley of the Mississippi, had now fairly begun. It would be more than seven years before it came to an end.

But most of the fighting was done at the north—in New York and Canada; and so Washington and his Virginian soldiers did not distinguish themselves in any very great enterprise.

It was for them to keep watch of the western frontier of the colony lest the Indians should cross the mountains and attack the settlements.

Once, near the middle of the war, Washington led a company into the very country where he had once traveled on foot with Christopher Gist.

The French had built a fort at the place where the Ohio River has its beginning, and they had named it Fort Duquesne. When they heard that Washington was coming they set fire to the fort and fled down the river in boats.

The English built a new fort at this same place, and called it Fort Pitt; and there the city of Pittsburgh has since grown up.

And now Washington resigned his commission as commander of the little Virginian army. Perhaps he was tired of the war. Perhaps his great plantation of Mount Vernon needed his care. We cannot tell.

But we know that, a few days later, he was married to Mrs. Martha Custis, a handsome young widow who owned a fine estate not a great way from Williamsburg, the capital of the colony. This was in January, 1759.

At about the same time he was elected a member of the House of Burgesses of Virginia; and three months later, he went down to Williamsburg to have a hand in making some of the laws for the colony.

He was now twenty-seven years old. Young as he was, he was one of the richest men in the colony, and he was known throughout the country as the bravest of American soldiers.

The war was still going on at the north. To most of the Virginians it seemed to be a thing far away.

At last, in 1763, a treaty of peace was made. The French had been beaten, and they were obliged to give up everything to the English. They lost not only the Ohio Country and all the great West, but Canada also.

The Mutterings of the Storm

And now for several years Washington lived the life of a country gentleman. He had enough to do, taking care of his plantations, hunting foxes with his sport-loving neighbors, and sitting for a part of each year in the House of Burgesses at Williamsburg.

He was a tall man—more than six feet in height. He had a commanding presence and a noble air, which plainly said: "This is no common man."

He was shrewd in business. He was the best horseman and the best walker in Virginia. And no man knew more about farming than he.

And so the years passed pleasantly enough at Mount Vernon, and there were few who dreamed of the great events and changes that were soon to take place.

King George the Third of England, who was the ruler of the thirteen colonies, had done many unwise things.

He had made laws forbidding the colonists from trading with other countries than his own.

He would not let them build factories to weave their wool and flax into cloth.

He wanted to force them to buy all their goods in England, and to send their corn and tobacco and cotton there to pay for them.

And now after the long war with France he wanted to make the colonists pay heavy taxes in order to meet the expenses of that war.

They must not drink a cup of tea without first paying tax on it; they must not sign a deed or a note without first buying stamped paper on which to write it.

In every colony there was a great excitement on account of the tea tax and the stamp act, as it was called.

In the House of Burgesses at Williamsburg, a young man, whose name was Patrick Henry, made a famous speech in which he declared that the king had no right to tax them without their consent.

George Washington heard that speech, and gave it his approval.

Not long afterward, news came that in Boston a shipload of tea had been thrown into the sea by the colonists. Rather than pay the tax upon it, they would drink no tea.

Then, a little later, still other news came. The king had closed the port of Boston, and would not allow any ships to come in or go out.

More than this, he had sent over a body of soldiers, and had quartered them in Boston in order to keep the people in subjection.

The whole country was aroused now. What did this mean? Did the king intend to take away from the colonists all the liberties that are so dear to men?

GEORGE WASHINGTON

The colonists must unite and agree upon doing something to protect themselves and preserve their freedom. In order to do this each colony was asked to send delegates to Philadelphia to talk over the matter and see what would be the best thing to do.

George Washington was one of the delegates from Virginia.

Before starting he made a great speech in the House of Burgesses. "If necessary, I will raise a thousand men," he said, "subsist them at my own expense, and march them to the relief of Boston."

But the time for marching to Boston had not quite come.

The delegates from the different colonies met in Carpenter's Hall, in Philadelphia, on the 5th of September, 1774. Their meeting has since been known as the First Continental Congress of America.

For fifty-one days those wise, thoughtful men discussed the great question that had brought them together. What could the colonists do to escape the oppressive laws that the King of England was trying to force upon them?

Many powerful speeches were made, but George Washington sat silent. He was a doer rather than a talker.

At last the Congress decided to send an address to the king to remind him of the rights of the colonists, and humbly beg that he would not enforce his unjust laws.

FOUR GREAT AMERICANS

And then, when all had been done that could be done, Washington went back to his home at Mount Vernon, to his family and his friends, his big plantations, his fox-hunting, and his pleasant life as a country gentleman.

But he knew as well as any man that more serious work was near at hand.

The Beginning of the War

All that winter the people of the colonies were anxious and fearful. Would the king pay any heed to their petition? Or would he force them to obey his unjust laws?

Then, in the spring, news came from Boston that matters were growing worse and worse. The soldiers who were quartered in that city were daily becoming more insolent and overbearing.

"These people ought to have their town knocked about their ears and destroyed," said one of the king's officers.

On the 19th of April a company of the king's soldiers started to Concord, a few miles from Boston, to seize some powder which had been stored there. Some of the colonists met them at Lexington, and there was a battle.

This was the first battle in that long war commonly called the Revolution.

Washington was now on his way to the North again. The Second Continental Congress was to meet in Philadelphia in May, and he was again a delegate from Virginia.

In the first days of the Congress no man was busier than he. No man seemed to understand the situation of things better than he. No man was listened to with greater respect; and yet he said but little.

Every day, he came into the hall wearing the blue and buff uniform which belonged to him as a Virginia colonel. It was as much as to say: "The time for fighting has come, and I am ready."

The Congress thought it best to send another humble petition to the king, asking him not to deprive the people of their just rights.

In the meantime brave men were flocking towards Boston to help the people defend themselves from the violence of the king's soldiers. The war had begun, and no mistake.

The men of Congress saw now the necessity of providing for this war. They asked, "Who shall be the commander-in-chief of our colonial army?"

It was hardly worth while to ask such a question; for there could be but one answer. Who, but George Washington?

No other person in America knew so much about war as he. No other person was so well fitted to command.

On the 15th of June, on motion of John Adams of Massachusetts, he was appointed to that responsible place. On the next day he made a modest but noble little speech before Congress.

He told the members of that body that he would serve his country willingly and as well as he could—but not for money. They might provide for his necessary expenses, but he would never take any pay for his services.

And so, leaving all his own interests out of sight, he undertook at once the great work that had been entrusted to him. He undertook it, not for profit nor for honor, but because of a feeling of duty to his fellowmen. For eight weary years he forgot himself in the service of his country.

Two weeks after his appointment General Washington rode into Cambridge, near Boston, and took formal command of his army.

It was but a small force, poorly clothed, poorly armed; but every man had the love of country in his heart. It was the first American army.

But so well did Washington manage matters that soon his raw troops were in good shape for service. And so hard did he press the king's soldiers in Boston that, before another summer, they were glad to take ship and sail away from the town which they had so long infested and annoyed.

Independence

On the fourth day of the following July there was a great stir in the town of Philadelphia. Congress was sitting in the Hall of the State House. The streets were full of people; everybody seemed anxious; everybody was in suspense.

Men were crowding around the State House and listening.

"Who is speaking now?" asked one.

"John Adams," was the answer.

"And who is speaking now?"

"Doctor Franklin."

"Good! Let them follow his advice, for he knows what is best."

Then there was a lull outside, for everybody wanted to hear what the great Dr. Franklin had to say.

After a while the same question was asked again; "Who is speaking now?"

And the answer was: "Thomas Jefferson of Virginia. It was he and Franklin who wrote it."

"Wrote what?"

"Why, the Declaration of Independence, of course."

A little later some one said: "They will be ready to sign it soon."

"But will they dare to sign it?"

"Dare? They dare not do otherwise."

Inside the hall grave men were discussing the acts of the King of England.

"He has cut off our trade with all parts of the world," said one.

"He has forced us to pay taxes without our consent," said another.

"He has sent his soldiers among us to burn our towns and kill our people," said a third.

"He has tried to make the Indians our enemies," said a fourth.

"He is a tyrant and unfit to be the ruler of a free people," they all agreed.

And then everybody was silent while one read: "We, therefore, the representatives of the United States of America, solemnly publish and declare that the united colonies are, and of right ought to be, *free and independent states.*"

Soon afterward the bell in the high tower above the hall began to ring.

"It is done!" cried the people. "They have signed the Declaration of Independence."

"Yes, every colony has voted for it," said those nearest the door. "The King of England shall no longer rule over us."

And that was the way in which the United States came into being. The thirteen colonies were now thirteen states.

Up to this time Washington and his army had been fighting for the rights of the people as colonists. They had been fighting in order to oblige the king to do away with the unjust laws which he had made. But now they were to fight for freedom and for the independence of the United States.

By and by you will read in your histories how wisely and bravely Washington conducted the war. You will learn how he held out against the king's soldiers on Long Island and at White Plains; how he crossed the Delaware amid floating ice and drove the English from Trenton; how he wintered at Morristown; how he suffered at Valley Forge; how he fought at Germantown and Monmouth and Yorktown.

There were six years of fighting, of marching here and there, of directing and planning, of struggling in the face of every discouragement.

Eight years passed, and then peace came, for independence had been won, and this our country was made forever free.

On the 2nd of November, 1783, Washington bade farewell to his army. On the 23d of December he resigned his commission as commander-in-chief.

There were some who suggested that Washington should make himself king of this country; and indeed this he might have done, so great was the people's love and gratitude.

But the great man spurned such suggestions. He said, "If you have any regard for your country or respect for me, banish those thoughts and never again speak of them."

The First President

Washington was now fifty-two years old.

The country was still in an unsettled condition. True, it was free from English control. But there was no strong government to hold the states together.

Each state was a little country of itself, making its own laws, and having its own selfish aims without much regard for its sister states. People did not think of the United States as one great undivided nation.

And so matters were in bad enough shape, and they grew worse and worse as the months went by.

Wise men saw that unless something should be done to bring about a closer union of the states, they would soon be in no better condition that when ruled by the English king.

And so a great convention was held in Philadelphia to determine what could be done to save the country from ruin. George Washington was chosen to preside over this convention; and no man's words had greater weight than his.

He said, "Let us raise a standard to which the wise and honest can repair. The event is in the hand of God."

That convention did a great and wonderful work; for it framed the Constitution by which our country has ever since been governed.

And soon afterward, in accordance with that Constitution, the people of the country were called upon to elect a President. Who should it be?

Who could it be but Washington?

When the electoral votes were counted, every vote was for George Washington of Virginia.

And so, on the 16th of April, 1789, the great man again bade adieu to Mount Vernon and to private life, and set out for New York. For the city of Washington had not yet been built, and New York was the first capital of our country.

There were no railroads at that time, and so the journey was made in a coach. All along the road the people gathered to see their hero-president and show him their love.

On the 30th of April he was inaugurated at the old Federal Hall in New York.

"Long live George Washington, President of the United States!" shouted the people. Then the cannon roared, the bells rang, and the new government of the United States—the government which we have to-day—began its existence.

Washington was fifty-seven years old at the time of his inauguration.

Perhaps no man was ever called to the doing of more difficult things. The entire government must be built up from the beginning, and all its machinery put into order.

But so well did he meet the expectations of the people, that when his first term was near its close he was again elected President, receiving every electoral vote.

In your histories you will learn of the many difficult tasks which he performed during those years of the nation's infancy. There were new troubles with England, troubles with the Indians, jealousies and disagreements among the law-makers of the country. But amidst all these trials Washington stood steadfast, wise, cool—conscious that he was right, and strong enough to prevail.

Before the end of his second term, people began to talk about electing him for the third time. They could not think of any other man holding the highest office in the country. They feared that no other man could be safely entrusted with the great responsibilities which he had borne so nobly.

But Washington declared that he would not accept office again. The government was now on a firm footing. There were others who could manage its affairs wisely and well.

And so, in September, 1796, he published his Farewell Address. It was full of wise and wholesome advice.

"Beware of attacks upon the Constitution. Beware of those who think more of their party than of their country. Promote education. Observe justice. Treat with good faith all nations. Adhere to the right. Be united—be united. Love your country." These were some of the things that he said.

John Adams, who had been vice-president eight years, was chosen to be the new President, and Washington again retired to Mount Vernon.

"First in War, First in Peace"

In the enjoyment of his home life, Washington did not forget his country. It would, indeed, have been hard for him not to keep informed about public affairs; for men were all the time coming to him to ask for help and advice regarding this measure or that.

The greatest men of the nation felt that he must know what was wisest and best for the country's welfare.

Soon after his retirement an unexpected trouble arose. There was another war between England and France. The French were very anxious that the United States should join in the quarrel.

GEORGE WASHINGTON

When they could not bring this about by persuasion, they tried abuse. They insulted the officers of our government; they threatened war.

The whole country was aroused. Congress began to take steps for the raising of an army and the building of a navy. But who should lead the army?

All eyes were again turned toward Washington. He had saved the country once; he could save it again. The President asked him if he would again be the commander-in-chief.

He answered that he would do so, on condition that he might choose his assistants. But unless the French should actually invade this country, he must not be expected to go into the field.

And so, at the last, General Washington is again the commander-in-chief of the American army. But there is to be no fighting this time. The French see that the people of the United States cannot be frightened; they see that the government cannot be driven; they leave off their abuse, and are ready to make friends.

Washington's work is done now. On the 12th of December, 1799, he mounts his horse and rides out over his farms. The weather is cold; the snow is falling; but he stays out for two or three hours.

The next morning he has a sore throat; he has taken cold. The snow is still falling, but he will go out again. At night he is very hoarse; he is advised to take medicine.

"Oh, no," he answers, "you know I never take anything for a cold."

But in the night he grows much worse; early the next morning the doctor is brought. It is too late. He grows rapidly worse. He knows that the end is near.

"It is well," he says; and these are his last words.

Washington died on the 14th of December, 1799. He had lived nearly sixty-eight years.

His sudden death was a shock to the entire country. Every one felt as though he had lost a personal friend. The mourning for him was general and sincere.

In the Congress of the United States his funeral oration was pronounced by his friend, Henry Lee, who said:

"First in war, first in peace, and first in the hearts of his countrymen, he was second to none in the humble and endearing scenes of private life. Pious, just, humane, temperate, uniform, dignified, and commanding, his example was edifying to all around him, as were the effects of that example lasting.

"Such was the man America has lost! Such was the man for whom our country mourns!"

THE STORY OF
BENJAMIN FRANKLIN

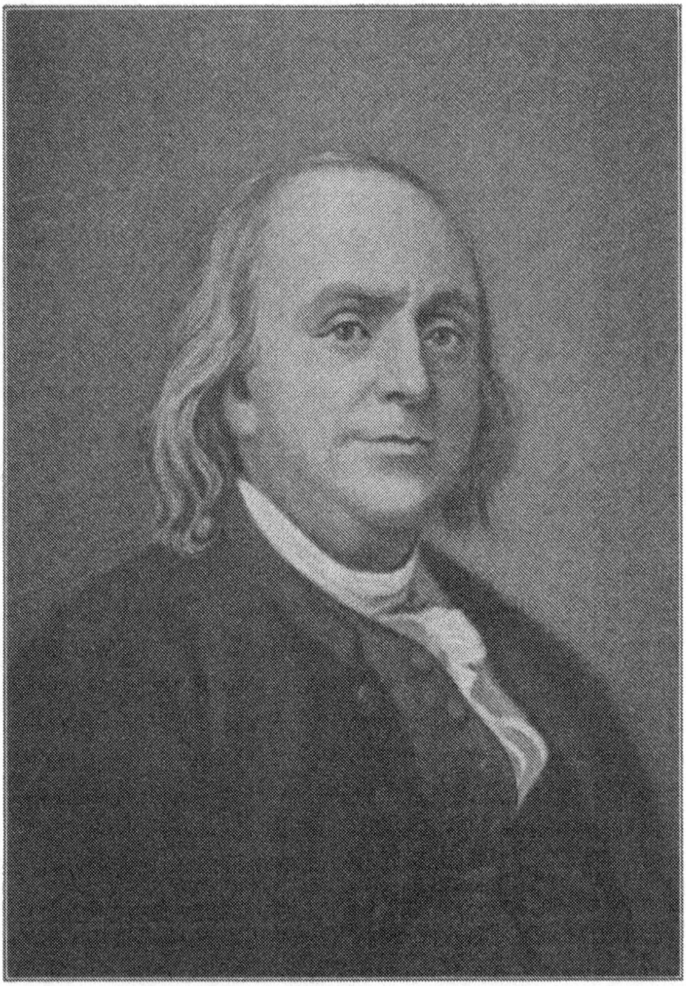

Benj. Franklin

THE STORY OF BENJAMIN FRANKLIN

The Whistle

Nearly two hundred years ago, there lived in Boston a little boy whose name was Benjamin Franklin.

On the day that he was seven years old, his mother gave him a few pennies.

He looked at the bright, yellow pieces and said, "What shall I do with these coppers, mother?"

It was the first money that he had ever had.

"You may buy something with them, if you would like," said his mother.

"And will you give me more when they are gone?" he asked.

His mother shook her head and said: "No, Benjamin. I cannot give you any more. So you must be careful not to spend them foolishly."

The little fellow ran out into the street. He heard the pennies jingle in his pocket as he ran. He felt as though he was very rich.

Boston was at that time only a small town, and there were not many stores. As Benjamin ran down toward the busy part of the street, he wondered what he should buy.

Should he buy candy or toys? It had been a long time since he had tasted candy. As for toys, he hardly knew what they were.

If he had been the only child in the family, things might have been different. But there were fourteen boys and girls older than he, and two little sisters that were younger.

It was as much as his father could do to earn food and clothing for so many. There was no money to spend for toys.

Before Benjamin had gone very far he met a boy blowing a whistle.

"That is just the thing that I want," he said. Then he hurried on to the store where all kinds of things were kept for sale.

"Have you any good whistles?" he asked.

He was out of breath from running, but he tried hard to speak like a man.

"Yes, plenty of them," said the man.

"Well, I want one, and I'll give you all the money I have for it," said the little fellow. He forgot to ask the price.

"How much money have you?" asked the man.

Benjamin took the coppers from his pocket. The man counted them and said, "All right, my boy. It's a bargain."

Then he put the pennies into his money drawer, and gave one of the whistles to the boy.

Benjamin Franklin was a proud and happy boy. He ran home as fast as he could, blowing his whistle as he ran.

His mother met him at the door and said, "Well, my child, what did you do with your pennies?"

"I bought a whistle!" he cried. "Just hear me blow it!"

"How much did you pay for it?"

"All the money I had."

One of his brothers was standing by and asked to see the whistle. "Well, well!" he said, "did you spend all of your money for this thing?"

"Every penny," said Benjamin.

"Did you ask the price?"

"No. But I offered them to the man, and he said it was all right."

His brother laughed and said, "You are a very foolish fellow. You paid four times as much as it is worth."

"Yes," said his mother, "I think it is rather a dear whistle. You had enough money to buy a whistle and some candy, too."

The little boy saw what a mistake he had made. The whistle did not please him any more. He threw it upon the floor, and began to cry. But his mother took him upon her lap and said: "Never mind, my child. We must all live and learn; and I think that my little boy will be careful, after this, not to pay too dear for his whistles."

Schooldays

When Benjamin Franklin was a boy there were no great public schools in Boston as there are now. But he learned to read almost as soon as he could talk, and he was always fond of books.

His nine brothers were older than he, and every one had learned a trade. They did not care so much for books.

"Benjamin shall be the scholar of our family," said his mother.

"Yes, we will educate him for a minister," said his father. For at that time all the most learned men were ministers.

And so, when he was eight years old, Benjamin Franklin was sent to a grammar school, where boys were prepared for college. He was a very apt scholar, and in a few months was promoted to a higher class.

But the lad was not allowed to stay long in the grammar school. His father was a poor man. It would cost a great deal of money to give Benjamin a college education. The times were very hard. The idea of educating the boy for the ministry had to be given up.

In less than a year he was taken from the grammar school, and sent to another school where arithmetic and writing were taught.

He learned to write very well, indeed; but he did not care so much for arithmetic, and so failed to do what was expected of him.

When he was ten years old he had to leave school altogether. His father needed his help; and though Benjamin was but a small boy, there were many things that he could do.

He never attended school again. But he kept on studying and reading; and we shall find that he afterwards became the most learned man in America.

Benjamin's father was a soap-boiler and candle-maker. And so when the boy was taken from school, what kind of work do you think he had to do?

He was kept busy cutting wicks for the candles, pouring the melted tallow into the candle-moulds, and selling soap to his father's customers.

Do you suppose that he liked this business?

He did not like it at all. And when he saw the ships sailing in and out of Boston harbor, he longed to be a sailor and go to strange, far-away lands, where candles and soap were unknown.

But his father would not listen to any of his talk about going to sea.

The Boys and the Wharf

Busy as Benjamin was in his father's shop, he still had time to play a good deal.

He was liked by all the boys of the neighborhood, and they looked up to him as their leader. In all their games he was their captain; and nothing was undertaken without asking his advice.

Not far from the home of the Franklins there was a mill pond, where the boys often went to swim. When the tide was high they liked to stand at a certain spot on the shore of the pond and fish for minnows.

But the ground was marshy and wet, and the boys' feet sank deep in the mud.

"Let us build a wharf along the water's edge," said Benjamin. "Then we can stand and fish with some comfort."

"Agreed!" said the boys. "But what is the wharf to be made of?"

Benjamin pointed to a heap of stones that lay not far away. They had been hauled there only a few days before, and were to be used in building a new house near the mill pond.

The boys needed only a hint. Soon they were as busy as ants, dragging the stones to the water's edge.

Before it was fully dark that evening, they had built a nice stone wharf on which they could stand and fish without danger of sinking in the mud.

The next morning the workmen came to begin the building of the house. They were surprised to find all the stones gone from the place where they had been thrown. But the tracks of the boys in the mud told the story.

It was easy enough to find out who had done the mischief.

When the boys' fathers were told of the trouble which they had caused, you may imagine what they did.

Young Benjamin Franklin tried hard to explain that a wharf on the edge of the mill pond was a public necessity.

His father would not listen to him. He said, "My son, nothing can ever be truly useful which is not at the same time truly honest."

And Benjamin never forgot this lesson.

Choosing a Trade

As I have already said, young Benjamin did not like the work which he had to do in his father's shop.

His father was not very fond of the trade himself, and so he could not blame the boy. One day he said:

Benjamin, since you have made up your mind not to be a candle-maker, what trade do you think you would like to learn?"

"You know I would like to be a sailor," said the boy.

"But you shall not be a sailor," said his father. "I intend that you shall learn some useful business on land; and, of course, you will succeed best in that kind of business which is most pleasant to you."

The next day he took the boy to walk with him among the shops of Boston. They saw all kinds of workmen busy at their various trades.

Benjamin was delighted. Long afterwards, when he had become a very great man, he said, "It has ever since been a pleasure to me to see good workmen handle their tools."

He gave up the thought of going to sea, and said that he would learn any trade that his father would choose for him.

His father thought that the cutler's trade was a good one. His cousin, Samuel Franklin, had just set up a cutler's shop in Boston, and he agreed to take Benjamin a few days on trial.

Benjamin was pleased with the idea of learning how to make knives and scissors and razors and all other kinds of cutting tools. But his cousin wanted so much money for teaching him the trade that his father could not afford it; and so the lad was taken back to the candle-maker's shop.

Soon after this, Benjamin's brother, James Franklin, set up a printing press in Boston. He intended to print and publish books and a newspaper.

"Benjamin loves books," said his father. "He shall learn to be a printer."

And so, when he was twelve years old, he was bound to his brother to learn the printer's trade. He was to stay with him until he was twenty-one. He was to have his board and clothing and no other wages, except during the last year. I suppose that during the last year he was to be paid the same as any other workman.

How Franklin Educated Himself

When Benjamin Franklin was a boy there were no books for children. Yet he spent most of his spare time in reading.

His father's books were not easy to understand. People nowadays would think them very dull and heavy.

But before he was twelve years old, Benjamin had read the most of them. He read everything that he could get.

After he went to work for his brother he found it easier to obtain good books. Often he would borrow a book in the evening, and then sit up nearly all night reading it so as to return it in the morning.

FOUR GREAT AMERICANS

Birthplace of Franklin
Boston U.S.

Press at which
Franklin worked

When the owners of books found that he always returned them soon and clean, they were very willing to lend him whatever he wished.

He was about fourteen years of age when he began to study how to write clearly and correctly. He afterwards told how he did this. He said:

"About this time I met with an odd volume of the *Spectator*. I had never before seen any of them.

"I bought it, read it over and over, and was much delighted with it.

"I thought the writing excellent, and wished if possible to imitate it.

"With that view, I took some of the papers, and making short hints of the sentiments in each sentence, laid them by a few days, and then, without looking at the book, tried to complete the papers again, by expressing each hinted sentiment at length and as fully as it had been expressed before, in any suitable words that should occur to me.

"Then I compared my *Spectator* with the original, discovered some of my faults and corrected them.

"But I found that I wanted a stock of words, or a readiness in recollecting and using them.

"Therefore, I took some of the tales in the *Spectator* and turned them into verse; and, after a time, when I had pretty well forgotten the prose, turned them back again."

About this time his brother began to publish a newspaper.

It was the fourth newspaper published in America, and was called the *New England Courant*.

People said that it was a foolish undertaking. They said that one newspaper was enough for this country, and that there would be but little demand for more.

In those days editors did not dare to write freely about public affairs. It was dangerous to criticise men who were in power.

James Franklin published something in the *New England Courant* about the lawmakers of Massachusetts. It made the lawmakers very angry. They caused James Franklin to be shut up in prison for a month, and they ordered that he should no longer print the newspaper called the *New England Courant*.

But, in spite of this order, the newspaper was printed every week as before. It was printed, however, in the name of Benjamin Franklin. For several years it bore his name as editor and publisher.

Farewell to Boston

Benjamin Franklin did not have a very happy life with his brother James.

His brother was a hard master, and was always finding fault with his workmen. Sometimes he would beat young Benjamin and abuse him without cause.

When Benjamin was nearly seventeen years old he made up his mind that he would not endure this treatment any longer.

He told his brother that he would leave him and find work with some one else.

When his brother learned that he really meant to do this, he went round to all the other printers in Boston and persuaded them not to give Benjamin any work.

The father took James's part, and scolded Benjamin for being so saucy and so hard to please. But Benjamin would not go back to James's printing house.

He made up his mind that since he could not find work in Boston he would run away from his home. He would go to New York and look for work there.

He sold his books to raise a little money. Then, without saying good-bye to his father or mother or any of his brothers or sisters, he went on board a ship that was just ready to sail from the harbor.

It is not likely that he was very happy while doing this. Long afterwards he said: "I reckon this as one of the first *errata* of my life."

What did he mean by *errata*?

Errata are mistakes—mistakes that cannot easily be corrected.

Three days after leaving Boston, young Franklin found himself in New York. It was then October, in the year 1723.

The lad had but very little money in his pocket. There was no one in New York that he knew. He was three hundred miles from home and friends.

As soon as he landed he went about the streets looking for work.

New York was only a little town then, and there was not a newspaper in it. There were but a few printing houses there, and these had not much work to do. The boy from Boston called at every place, but he found that nobody wanted to employ any more help.

At one of the little printing houses Franklin was told that perhaps he could find work in Philadelphia, which was at that time a much more important place than New York.

Philadelphia was one hundred miles farther from home. One hundred miles was a long distance in those days.

But Franklin made up his mind to go there without delay. It would be easier to do this than to give up and try to return to Boston.

BENJAMIN FRANKLIN

The First Day in Philadelphia

There are two ways of going from New York to Philadelphia.

One way is by the sea. The other is by land, across the state of New Jersey.

As Franklin had but little money, he took the shorter route by land; but he sent his little chest, containing his Sunday clothes, round by sea, in a boat.

He walked all the way from Perth Amboy, on the eastern shore of New Jersey, to Burlington, on the Delaware River.

Nowadays you may travel that distance in an hour, for it is only about fifty miles.

But there were no railroads at that time; and Franklin was nearly three days trudging along lonely wagon-tracks, in the midst of a pouring rain.

At Burlington he was lucky enough to be taken on board a small boat that was going down the river.

Burlington is only twenty miles above Philadelphia. But the boat moved very slowly, and as there was no wind, the men took turns at rowing.

Night came on, and they were afraid that they might pass by Philadelphia in the darkness. So they landed, and camped on shore till morning.

Early the next day they reached Philadelphia, and Benjamin Franklin stepped on shore at the foot of

Market Street, where the Camden ferry-boats now land.

No one who saw him could have guessed that he would one day be the greatest man in the city.

He was a sorry-looking fellow.

He was dressed in his working clothes, and was very dirty from being so long on the road and in the little boat.

His pockets were stuffed out with shirts and stockings, and all the money that he had was not more than a dollar.

He was hungry and tired. He had not a single friend. He did not know of any place where he could look for lodging.

It was Sunday morning.

He went a little way up the street, and looked around him.

A boy was coming down, carrying a basket of bread.

"My young friend," said Franklin, "where did you get that bread?"

"At the baker's," said the boy.

"And where is the baker's?"

The boy showed him the little baker shop just around the corner.

Young Franklin was so hungry that he could hardly wait. He hurried into the shop and asked for three-penny worth of bread.

BENJAMIN FRANKLIN

The baker gave him three great, puffy rolls. Franklin had not expected to get so much, but he took the rolls and walked out.

His pockets were already full, and so, while he ate one roll, he held the others under his arms.

As he went up Market Street, eating his roll, a young girl stood in a doorway laughing at him. He was, indeed, a very funny-looking fellow.

The girl's name was Deborah Read. A few years after that, she became the wife of Benjamin Franklin.

Hungry as he was, Franklin found that he could eat but one of the rolls, and so he gave the other two to a poor woman who had come down the river in the same boat with him.

As he was strolling along the street he came to a Quaker meetinghouse.

The door was open, and many people were sitting quietly inside. The seats looked inviting, and so Franklin walked in and sat down.

The day was warm; the people in the house were very still; Franklin was tired. In a few minutes he was sound asleep.

And so it was in a Quaker meetinghouse that Benjamin Franklin found the first shelter and rest in Philadelphia.

Later in the day, as Franklin was strolling toward the river, he met a young man whose honest face was very pleasing to him.

"My friend," he said, "can you tell me of any house where they lodge strangers?"

"Yes," said the young man, "there is a house on this very street; but it is not a place I can recommend. If thee will come with me I will show thee a better one."

Franklin walked with him to a house on Water Street, and there he found lodging for the night.

And so ended his first day in Philadelphia.

Governor William Keith

Franklin soon obtained work in a printing house owned by a man named Keimer.

He found a boarding place in the house of Mr. Read, the father of the girl who had laughed at him with his three rolls.

He was only seventeen years old, and he soon became acquainted with several young people in the town who loved books.

In a little while he began to lay up money, and he tried to forget his old home in Boston as much as he could.

One day a letter came to Philadelphia for Benjamin Franklin.

It was from Captain Robert Holmes, a brother-in-law of Franklin's.

Captain Holmes was the master of a trading sloop that sailed between Boston and Delaware Bay. While he was loading his vessel at Newcastle, forty miles below Philadelphia, he had happened to hear about the young man Franklin who had lately come from Boston.

He sat down at once and wrote a letter to the young man. He told him how his parents and friends were grieving for him in Boston. He begged him to go back home, and said that everything would be made right if he would do so.

When Franklin read this letter he felt very sad to think of the pain and distress which he had caused.

But he did not want to return to Boston. He felt that he had been badly treated by his brother, and, therefore, that he was not the only one to be blamed. He believed that he could do much better in Philadelphia than anywhere else.

So he sat down and wrote an answer to Captain Holmes. He wrote it with great care, and sent it off to Newcastle by the first boat that was going that way.

Now it so happened that Sir William Keith, the governor of the province, was at Newcastle at that very time. He was with Captain Holmes when the letter came to hand.

When Captain Holmes had read the letter he was so pleased with it that he showed it to the governor.

Governor Keith read it and was surprised when he learned that its writer was a lad only seventeen years old.

"He is a young man of great promise," he said; "and he must be encouraged. The printers in Philadelphia know nothing about their business. If young Franklin will stay there and set up a press, I will do a great deal for him."

One day not long after that, when Franklin was at work in Keimer's printing-office, the governor came to see him. Franklin was very much surprised.

The governor offered to set him up in a business of his own. He promised that he should have all the public printing in the province.

"But you will have to go to England to buy your types and whatever else you may need."

Franklin agreed to do this. But he must first return to Boston and get his father's consent and assistance.

The governor gave him a letter to carry to his father. In a few weeks he was on his way home.

You may believe that Benjamin's father and mother were glad to see him. He had been gone seven months, and in all that time they had not heard a word from him.

His brothers and sisters were glad to see him, too—all but the printer, James, who treated him very unkindly.

His father read the governor's letter, and then shook his head.

"What kind of a man is this Governor Keith?" he asked. "He must have but little judgment to think of setting up a mere boy in business of this kind."

After that he wrote a letter of thanks to the governor. He said that he was grateful for the kindness he had shown to his son, and for his offer to help him. But he thought that Benjamin was still too young to be trusted with so great a business, and therefore he would not consent to his undertaking it. As for helping him, that he could not do; for he had but little more money than was needed to carry on his own affairs.

The Return to Philadelphia

Benjamin Franklin felt much disappointed when his father refused to help send him to England. But he was not discouraged.

In a few weeks he was ready to return to Philadelphia. This time he did not have to run away from home.

His father blessed him, and his mother gave him many small gifts as tokens of her love.

"Be diligent," said his father, "attend well to your business, and save your money carefully, and, perhaps, by the time you are twenty-one years old, you will be able to set up for yourself without the governor's help."

All the family, except James the printer, bade him a kind good-bye, as he went on board the little ship that was to take him as far as New York.

There was another surprise for him when he reached New York.

The governor of New York had heard that there was a young man from Boston on board the ship, and that he had a great many books.

There were no large libraries in New York at that time. There were no bookstores, and but few people who cared for books.

So the governor sent for Franklin to come and see him. He showed him his own library, and they had a long talk about books and authors.

This was the second governor that had taken notice of Benjamin. For a poor boy, like him, it was a great honor, and very pleasing.

When he arrived in Philadelphia he gave to Governor Keith the letter which his father had written.

The governor was not very well pleased. He said:

"Your father is too careful. There is a great difference in persons. Young men can sometimes be trusted with great undertakings as well as if they were older."

He then said that he would set Franklin up in business without his father's help.

"Give me a list of everything needed in a first-class printing-office. I will see that you are properly fitted out."

Franklin was delighted. He thought that Governor Keith was one of the best men in the world.

In a few days he laid before the governor a list of the things needed in a little printing-office.

The cost of the outfit would be about five hundred dollars.

The governor was pleased with the list. There were no type-foundries in America at that time. There was no place where printing-presses were made. Everything had to be bought in England.

The governor said, "Don't you think it would be better if you could go to England and choose the types for yourself, and see that everything is just as you would like to have it?"

"Yes, sir," said Franklin, "I think that would be a great advantage."

"Well, then," said the governor, "get yourself ready to go on the next regular ship to London. It shall be at my expense."

At that time there was only one ship that made regular trips from Philadelphia to England, and it sailed but once each year.

The name of this ship was the *Annis*. It would not be ready to sail again for several months.

And so young Franklin, while he was getting ready for the voyage, kept on working in Mr. Keimer's little printing-office.

He laid up money enough to pay for his passage. He did not want to be dependent upon Governor Keith for everything; and it was well that he did not.

The First Visit to England

At last the *Annis* was ready to sail.

Governor Keith had promised to give to young Franklin letters of introduction to some of his friends in England.

He had also promised to give him money to buy his presses and type.

But when Franklin called at the governor's house to bid him good-bye, and to get the letters, the governor was too busy to see him. He said that he would send the letters and the money to him on shipboard.

The ship sailed.

But no letters, nor any word from Governor Keith, had been sent to Franklin.

When he at last arrived in London he found himself without money and without friends.

Governor Keith had given him nothing but promises. He would never give him anything more. He was a man whose word was not to be depended upon.

Franklin was then just eighteen years old. He must now depend wholly upon himself. He must make his own way in the world, without aid from anyone.

He went out at once to look for work. He found employment in a printing-office, and there he stayed for nearly a year.

Franklin made many acquaintances with literary people while he was in London.

He proved himself to be a young man of talent and ingenuity. He was never idle.

His companions in the printing-office were beer-drinkers and sots. He often told them how foolish they were to spend their money and ruin themselves for drink.

He drank nothing but water. He was strong and active. He could carry more, and do more work, than any of them.

He persuaded many of them to leave off drinking, and to lead better lives.

Franklin was also a fine swimmer. There was no one in London who could swim as well. He wrote two essays on swimming, and made some plans for opening a swimming school.

When he had been in London about a year, he met a Mr. Denham, a merchant of Philadelphia, and a strong friendship sprang up between them.

Mr. Denham at last persuaded Franklin to return to Philadelphia, and be a clerk in his dry-goods store.

And so, on the 23rd of the next July, he set sail for home. The ship was nearly three months in making the voyage, and it was not until October that he again set foot in Philadelphia.

A Leading Man in Philadelphia

When Franklin was twenty-four years old he was married to Miss Deborah Read, the young lady who had laughed at him when he was walking the street with his three rolls.

They lived together very happily for a great many years.

Some time before this marriage, Franklin's friend and employer, Mr. Denham, had died.

The dry-goods store, of which he was the owner, had been sold, and Franklin's occupation as a salesman, or clerk, was gone. But the young man had shown himself to be a person of great industry and ability. He had the confidence of everybody that knew him.

A friend of his, who had money, offered to take him as a partner in the newspaper business. And so he again became a printer, and the editor of a paper called the *Pennsylvania Gazette*.

BENJAMIN FRANKLIN

It was not long until Franklin was recognized as one of the leading men in Philadelphia. His name was known, not only in Pennsylvania, but in all the colonies.

He was all the time thinking of plans for making the people about him wiser and better and happier.

He established a subscription and circulating library, the first in America. This library was the beginning of the present Philadelphia Public Library.

He wrote papers on education. He founded the University of Pennsylvania. He organized the American Philosophical Society.

He established the first fire company in Philadelphia, which was also the first in America.

He invented a copper-plate press, and printed the first paper money of New Jersey.

He also invented the iron fireplace, which is called the Franklin stove, and is still used where wood is plentiful and cheap.

After an absence of ten years, he paid a visit to his old home in Boston. Everybody was glad to see him now,—even his brother James, the printer.

When he returned to Philadelphia, he was elected clerk of the colonial assembly.

Not long after that, he was chosen to be postmaster of the city. But his duties in this capacity did not require very much labor in those times.

He did not handle as much mail in a whole year as passes now through the Philadelphia post-office in a single hour.

Franklin's Rules of Life

Here are some of the rules of life which Franklin made for himself when he was a very young man:

1. To live very frugally till he had paid all that he owed.

2. To speak the truth at all times; to be sincere in word and action.

3. To apply himself earnestly to whatever business he took in hand; and to shun all foolish projects for becoming suddenly rich. "For industry and patience," he said, "are the surest means of plenty."

4. To speak ill of no man whatever, not even in a matter of truth; but to speak all the good he knew of everybody.

When he was twenty-six years old, he published the first number of an almanac called *Poor Richard's Almanac*.

This almanac was full of wise and witty sayings, and everybody soon began to talk about it.

Every year, for twenty-five years, a new number of *Poor Richard's Almanac* was printed. It was sold in all parts of the country. People who had no other books would buy and read *Poor Richard's Almanac*. The library of many a farmer consisted of only the family Bible with one or more numbers of this famous almanac.

Here are a few of Poor Richard's sayings:

"A word to the wise is enough."

"God helps them that help themselves."

"Early to bed and early to rise,
 Makes a man healthy, wealthy, and wise."

"There are no gains without pains."

"Plow deep while sluggards sleep,
 And you shall have corn to sell and to keep."

"One to-day is worth two to-morrows."

"Little strokes fell great oaks."

"Keep thy shop and thy shop will keep thee."

"The sleeping fox catches no poultry."

"Diligence is the mother of good luck."

"Constant dropping wears away stones."

"A small leak will sink a great ship."

"Who dainties love shall beggars prove."

"Creditors have better memories than debtors."

"Many a little makes a mickle."

"Fools make feasts and wise men eat them."

"Many have been ruined by buying good pennyworths."

"Rather go to bed supperless than rise in debt."

"For age and want save while you may;
No morning sun lasts the whole day."

It is pleasant to know that Franklin observed the rules of life which he made. And his wife, Deborah, was as busy and as frugal as himself.

They kept no idle servants. Their furniture was of the cheapest sort. Their food was plain and simple.

Franklin's breakfast, for many years, was only bread and milk; and he ate it out of a two-penny earthen bowl with a pewter spoon.

But at last, when he was called one morning to breakfast, he found his milk in a china bowl; and by the side of the bowl there was a silver spoon.

His wife had bought them for him as a surprise. She said that she thought her husband deserved a silver spoon and china bowl as well as any of his neighbors.

Franklin's Services to the Colonies

And so, as you have seen, Benjamin Franklin became in time one of the foremost men in our country.

In 1753, when he was forty-five years old, he was made deputy postmaster-general for America.

He was to have a salary of about $3,000 a year, and was to pay his own assistants.

People were astonished when he proposed to have the mail carried regularly once every week between New York and Boston.

Letters starting from Philadelphia on Monday morning would reach Boston the next Saturday night. This was thought to be a wonderful and almost impossible feat. But nowadays, letters leaving Philadelphia at midnight are read at the breakfast table in Boston the next morning.

At that time there were not seventy post-offices in the whole country. There are now more than seventy thousand.

Benjamin Franklin held the office of deputy postmaster-general for the American colonies for twenty-one years.

In 1754 there was a meeting of the leading men of all the colonies at Albany. There were fears of a war with the French and Indians of Canada, and the colonies had sent these men to plan some means of defence.

Benjamin Franklin was one of the men from Pennsylvania at this meeting.

He presented a plan for the union of the colonies, and it was adopted. But our English rulers said it was too democratic, and refused to let it go into operation.

This scheme of Franklin's set the people of the colonies to thinking. Why should the colonies not unite? Why should they not help one another, and thus form one great country?

And so, we may truthfully say that it was Benjamin Franklin who first put into men's minds the idea of the great Union which we now call the United States of America.

The people of the colonies were not happy under the rule of the English. One by one, laws were made which they looked upon as oppressive and burdensome. These laws were not intended to benefit the American people, but were designed to enrich the merchants and politicians of England.

In 1757 the people of Pennsylvania, Massachusetts, Maryland, and Georgia, decided to send some one to England to petition against these oppressions.

In all the colonies there was no man better fitted for this business than Benjamin Franklin. And so he was the man sent.

The fame of the great American had gone before him. Everybody seemed anxious to do him honor.

He met many of the leading men of the day, and he at last succeeded in gaining the object of his mission.

But such business moved slowly in those times. Five years passed before he was ready to return to America.

He reached Philadelphia in November, 1762, and the colonial assembly of Pennsylvania thanked him publicly for his great services.

But new troubles soon came up between the colonies and the government in England. Other laws were passed, more oppressive than before.

It was proposed to tax the colonies, and to force the colonists to buy stamped paper. This last act was called the Stamp Tax, and the American people opposed it with all their might.

Scarcely had Franklin been at home two years when he was again sent to England to plead the cause of his countrymen.

This time he remained abroad for more than ten years; but he was not so successful as before.

In 1774 he appeared before the King's council to present a petition from the people of Massachusetts.

He was now a venerable man nearly seventy years of age. He was the most famous man of America.

His petition was rejected. He himself was shamefully insulted and abused by one of the members of the council. The next day he was dismissed from the office of deputy postmaster-general of America.

In May, 1775, he was again at home in Philadelphia.

Two weeks before his arrival the battle of Lexington had been fought, and the war of the Revolution had been begun.

Franklin had done all that he could to persuade the English king to deal justly with the American colonies. But the king and his counselors had refused to listen to him.

During his ten years abroad he had not stayed all the time in England. He had traveled in many countries of Europe, and had visited Paris several times.

Many changes had taken place while he was absent.

His wife, Mrs. Deborah Franklin, had died. His parents and fifteen of his brothers and sisters had also been laid in the grave.

The rest of his days were to be spent in the service of his country, to which he had already given nearly twenty years of his life.

Franklin's Wonderful Kite

Benjamin Franklin was not only a printer, politician, and statesman, he was the first scientist of America. In the midst of perplexing cares it was his delight to study the laws of nature and try to understand some of the mysteries of creation.

In his time no very great discoveries had yet been made. The steam engine was unknown. The telegraph had not so much as been dreamed about. Thousands of comforts which we now enjoy through the discoveries of science were then unthought of; or if thought of, they were deemed to be impossible.

BENJAMIN FRANKLIN

Franklin began to make experiments in electricity when he was about forty years old.

He was the first person to discover that lightning is caused by electricity. He had long thought that this was true, but he had no means of proving it.

He thought that if he could stand on some high tower during a thunderstorm, he might be able to draw some of the electricity from the clouds through a pointed iron rod. But there was no high tower in Philadelphia. There was not even a tall church spire.

At last he thought of making a kite and sending it up to the clouds. A paper kite, however, would be ruined by the rain and would not fly to any great height.

So instead of paper he used a light silk handkerchief which he fastened to two slender but strong cross pieces. At the top of the kite he placed a pointed iron rod. The string was of hemp, except a short piece at the lower end, which was of silk. At the end of the hemp string an iron key was tied.

"I think that is a queer kind of kite," said Franklin's little boy. "What are you going to do with it?"

"Wait until the next thunderstorm, and you will see," said Franklin. "You may go with me and we will send it up to the clouds."

He told no one else about it, for if the experiment should fail, he did not care to have everybody laugh at him.

At last, one day, a thunderstorm came up, and Franklin, with his son, went out into a field to fly his kite. There was a steady breeze, and it was easy to send the kite far up towards the clouds.

Then, holding the silken end of the string, Franklin stood under a little shed in the field, and watched to see what would happen.

The lightnings flashed, the thunder rolled, but there was no sign of electricity in the kite. At last, when he was about to give up the experiment, Franklin saw the loose fibres of his hempen string begin to move.

He put his knuckles close to the key, and sparks of fire came flying to his hand. He was wild with delight. The sparks of fire were electricity; he had drawn them from the clouds.

That experiment, if Franklin had only known it, was a very dangerous one. It was fortunate for him, and for the world, that he suffered no harm. More than one person who has since tried to draw electricity from the clouds has been killed by the lightning that has flashed down the hempen kite string.

When Franklin's discovery was made known it caused great excitement among the learned men of Europe. They could not believe it was true until some of them had proved it by similar experiments.

They could hardly believe that a man in the far-away city of Philadelphia could make a discovery which they had never thought of as possible. Indeed, how could an American do anything that was worth doing.

Franklin soon became famous in foreign countries as a philosopher and man of science. The universities of Oxford and Edinburgh honored him by conferring upon him their highest degrees. He was now *Doctor* Benjamin Franklin. But in America people still thought of him only as a man of affairs, as a great printer, and as the editor of *Poor Richard's Almanac.*

All this happened before the beginning of his career as ambassador from the colonies to the king and government of England.

I cannot tell you of all of his discoveries in science. He invented the lightning rod, and, by trying many experiments, he learned more about electricity than the world had ever known before.

He made many curious experiments to discover the laws of heat, light, and sound. By laying strips of colored cloth on snow, he learned which colors are the best conductors of heat.

He invented the harmonica, an ingenious musical instrument, in which the sounds were produced by musical glasses.

During his long stay abroad he did not neglect his scientific studies. He visited many of the greatest scholars of the time, and was everywhere received with much honor.

The great scientific societies of Europe, the Royal Academies in Paris and in Madrid, had already elected him as one of their members. The King of France wrote him a letter, thanking him for his useful discoveries in electricity, and for his invention of the lightning rod.

All this would have made some men very proud. But it was not so with Dr. Franklin. In a letter which he wrote to a friend at the time when these honors were beginning to be showered upon him, he said:

"The pride of man is very differently gratified; and had his Majesty sent me a marshal's staff I think I should scarce have been so proud of it as I am of your esteem."

The Last Years

In 1776 delegates from all the colonies met in Philadelphia. They formed what is known in history as the Second Continental Congress of America.

It was now more than a year since the war had begun, and the colonists had made up their minds not to obey the oppressive laws of the King of England and his council.

Many of them were strongly in favor of setting up a new government of their own.

The Congress, therefore, appointed a committee to draft a declaration of independence. Benjamin Franklin was one of that committee.

On the 4th of July, Congress declared the colonies to be free and independent states, no longer subject to the laws of England. Among the men who signed their names to this Declaration of Independence was Benjamin Franklin of Pennsylvania.

Soon after this Dr. Franklin was sent to Paris as minister from the United States. Early in the following year, 1777, he induced the King of France to acknowledge the independence of this country.

He thus secured aid for the Americans at a time when they were in the greatest need of it. Had it not been for his services at this time, the war of the Revolution might have ended very differently, indeed.

It was not until 1785 that he was again able to return to his home.

He was then nearly eighty years old.

He had served his country faithfully for fifty-three years. He would have been glad if he might retire to private life, but the people who knew and appreciated his great worth, would not permit him to do so.

When he reached Philadelphia he was received with joy by thousands of his countrymen.

General Washington was among the first to welcome him, and to thank him for his great services.

That same year the grateful people of his state elected him President of Pennsylvania.

Two years afterwards, he wrote:

"I am here in my *niche* in my own house, in the bosom of my family, my daughter and grandchildren all about me, among my old friends, or the sons of my friends, who equally respect me.

"In short, I enjoy here every opportunity of doing good, and everything else I could wish for, except repose; and that I may soon expect, either by the cessation of my office, which cannot last more than three years, or by ceasing to live."

The next year he was a delegate to the convention which formed the present Constitution of the United States. By the adoption of this Constitution, the thirteen United States became a single nation worthy to be ranked with the other great governments of the world.

In a letter written to his friend, General Washington, not long afterwards, Benjamin Franklin said: "For my personal ease I should have died two years ago; but though those years have been spent in pain, I am glad to have lived them, since I can look upon our present situation."

In April, 1790, he died, and was buried by the side of his wife, Deborah, in Arch street graveyard in Philadelphia. His age was eighty-four years and three months.

Many years before his death he had written the following epitaph for himself:

BENJAMIN FRANKLIN

> "The Body
> of
> Benjamin Franklin, Printer,
> (Like the cover of an old book,
> Its contents torn out,
> And stripped of its lettering and gilding,)
> Lies here food for worms.
> Yet the work itself shall not be lost,
> For it will (as he believed) appear once more
> In a new
> And more beautiful Edition,
> Corrected and Amended
> By
> The Author."

THE STORY OF DANIEL WEBSTER

Danl Webster

THE STORY OF DANIEL WEBSTER

Captain Webster

Many years ago there lived in New Hampshire a poor farmer, whose name was Ebenezer Webster.

His little farm was among the hills, not far from the Merrimac River. It was a beautiful place to live in; but the ground was poor, and there were so many rocks that you would wonder how anything could grow among them.

Ebenezer Webster was known far and wide as a brave, wise man. When any of his neighbors were in trouble or in doubt about anything, they always said, "We will ask Captain Webster about it."

They called him Captain because he had fought the French and Indians and had been a brave soldier in the Revolutionary War. Indeed, he was one of the first men in New Hampshire to take up arms for his country.

When he heard that the British were sending soldiers to America to force the people to obey the unjust laws of the King of England, he said, "We must never submit to this."

So he went among his neighbors and persuaded them to sign a pledge to do all that they could to defend the country against the British. Then he raised a company of two hundred men and led them to Boston to join the American army.

The Revolutionary War lasted several years; and during all that time, Captain Webster was known as one of the bravest of the American patriots.

One day, at West Point, he met General Washington. The patriots were in great trouble at that time, for one of their leaders had turned traitor and had gone to help the British. The officers and soldiers were much distressed, for they did not know who might be the next to desert them.

As I have said, Captain Webster met General Washington. The general took the captain's hand, and said: "I believe that I can trust you, Captain Webster."

You may believe that this made Captain Webster feel very happy. When he went back to his humble home among the New Hampshire hills, he was never so proud as when telling his neighbors about this meeting with General Washington.

If you could have seen Captain Ebenezer Webster in those days, you would have looked at him more than once. He was a remarkable man. He was very tall and straight, with dark, glowing eyes, and hair as black as night. His face was kind, but it showed much firmness and decision.

He had never attended school; but he had tried, as well as he could, to educate himself. It was on account of his honesty and good judgment that he was looked up to as the leading man in the neighborhood.

In some way, I do not know how, he had gotten a little knowledge of the law. And at last, because of this as well as because of his sound common sense, he was appointed judge of the court in his county.

This was several years after the war was over. He was now no longer called Captain Webster, but Judge Webster.

It had been very hard for him to make a living for his large family on the stony farm among the hills. But now his office as judge would bring him three hundred or four hundred dollars a year. He had never had so much money in his life.

"Judge Webster," said one of his neighbors, "what are you going to do with the money that you get from your office? Going to build a new house?"

"Well, no," said the judge. "The old house is small, but we have lived in it a long time, and it still does very well."

"Then I suppose you are planning to buy more land?" said the neighbor.

"No, indeed, I have as much land now as I can cultivate. But I will tell you what I am going to do with my money, I am going to try to educate my boys. I would rather do this than have lands and houses."

The Youngest Son

Ebenezer Webster had several sons. But at the time that he was appointed judge there were only two at home. The older ones were grown up and were doing for themselves.

It was of the two at home that he was thinking when he said, "I am going to try to educate my boys."

Of the ten children in the family, the favorite was a black-haired, dark-skinned little fellow called Daniel. He was the youngest of all the boys; but there was one girl who was younger than he.

Daniel Webster was born on the 18th of January, 1782.

He was a puny child, very slender and weak; and the neighbors were fond of telling his mother that he could not live long. Perhaps this was one of the things that caused him to be favored and petted by his parents.

But there were other reasons why every one was attracted by him. There were other reasons why his brothers and sisters were always ready to do him a service.

He was an affectionate, loving child; and he was wonderfully bright and quick.

He was not strong enough to work on the farm like other boys. He spent much of his time playing in the woods or roaming among the hills.

And when he was not at play he was quite sure to be found in some quiet corner with a book in his hand. He afterwards said of himself: "In those boyish days there were two things that I dearly loved—reading and playing."

He could never tell how or when he had learned to read. Perhaps his mother had taught him when he was but a mere babe.

He was very young when he was first sent to school. The schoolhouse was two or three miles away, but he did not mind the long walk through the woods and over the hills.

It was not a great while until he had learned all that his teacher was able to teach him; for he had a quick understanding, and he remembered everything that he read.

The people of the neighborhood never tired of talking about "Webster's boy," as they called him. All agreed that he was a wonderful child.

Some said that so wonderful a child was sure to die young. Others said that if he lived he would certainly become a very great man.

When the farmers, on their way to market, drove past Judge Webster's house, they were always glad if they could see the delicate boy, with his great dark eyes.

If it was near the hour of noon, they would stop their teams under the shady elms and ask him to come out and read to them. Then, while their horses rested and ate, they would sit round the boy and listen to his wonderful tones as he read page after page from the Bible.

There were no children's books in those times. Indeed, there were very few books to be had of any kind. But young Daniel Webster found nothing too hard to read.

"I read what I could get to read," he afterwards said; "I went to school when I could, and when not at school, was a farmer's youngest boy, not good for much for want of health and strength, but expected to do something."

One day the man who kept the little store in the village, showed him something that made his heart leap.

It was a cotton handkerchief with the Constitution of the United States printed on one side of it.

In those days people were talking a great deal about the Constitution, for it had just then come into force.

Daniel had never read it. When he saw the handkerchief he could not rest till he had made it his own.

He counted all his pennies, he borrowed a few from his brother Ezekiel. Then he hurried back to the store and bought the wished-for treasure.

In a short time he knew everything in the Constitution, and could repeat whole sections of it from memory. We shall learn that, when he afterwards became one of the great men of this nation, he proved to be the Constitution's wisest friend and ablest defender.

Ezekiel and Daniel

Ezekiel Webster was two years older than his brother Daniel. He was a strong, manly fellow, and was ready at all times to do a kindness to the lad who had not been gifted with so much health and strength.

But he had not Daniel's quickness of mind, and he always looked to his younger brother for advice and instruction.

And so there was much love between the two brothers, each helping the other according to his talents and his ability.

One day they went together to the county fair. Each had a few cents in his pocket for spending-money, and both expected to have a fine time.

When they came home in the evening Daniel seemed very happy, but Ezekiel was silent.

"Well, Daniel," said their mother, "what did you do with your money?"

"I spent it at the fair," said Daniel.

"And what did you do with yours, Ezekiel?"

"I lent it to Daniel," was the answer.

It was this way at all times, and with everybody. Not only Ezekiel, but others were ever ready to give up their own means of enjoyment if only it would make Daniel happy.

At another time the brothers were standing together by their father, who had just come home after several days' absence.

"Ezekiel," said Mr. Webster, "what have you been doing since I went away?"

"Nothing, sir," said Ezekiel.

"You are very frank," said the judge. Then turning to Daniel, he said:

"What have you been doing, Dan?"

"Helping Zeke," said Daniel.

When Judge Webster said to his neighbor, "I am going to try to educate my boys," he had no thought of ever being able to send both of them to college.

Ezekiel, he said to himself, was strong and hearty. He could make his own way in the world without having a finished education.

But Daniel had little strength of body, although he was gifted with great mental powers. It was he that must be the scholar of the family.

The judge argued with himself that since he would be able to educate only one of the boys, he must educate that one who gave the greatest promise of success. And yet, had it not been for his poverty, he would gladly have given the same opportunities to both.

Plans for the Future

One hot day in summer the judge and his youngest son were at work together in the hayfield.

"Daniel," said the judge, "I am thinking that this kind of work is hardly the right thing for you. You must prepare yourself for greater things than pitching hay."

"What do you mean, father?" asked Daniel.

"I mean that you must have that which I have always felt the need of. You must have a good education; for without an education a man is always at a disadvantage. If I had been able to go to school when I was a boy, I might have done more for my country than I have. But as it is, I can do nothing but struggle here for the means of living."

"Zeke and I will help you, father," said Daniel; "and now that you are growing old, you need not work so hard."

"I am not complaining about the work," said the judge. "I live only for my children. When your older brothers were growing up I was too poor to give them an education; but I am able now to do something for you, and I mean to send you to a good school."

"Oh, father, how kind you are!" cried Daniel.

"If you will study hard," said his father—"if you will do your best, and learn all that you can, you will not have to endure such hardships as I have endured. And then you will be able to do so much more good in the world."

The boy's heart was touched by the manner in which his father spoke these words. He dropped his rake; he threw his arms around his father's neck, and cried for joy.

It was not until the next spring that Judge Webster felt himself able to carry out his plans to send Daniel to school.

One evening he said, "Daniel, you must be up early in the morning, I am going with you to Exeter."

"To Exeter?" said the boy.

"Yes, to Exeter. I am going to put you in the academy there."

The academy at Exeter was then, as it still is, a famous place for preparing boys for college. But Daniel's father did not say anything about making him ready for college. The judge knew that the expenses would be heavy, and he was not sure that he would ever be able to give him a finished education.

It was nearly fifty miles to Exeter, and Daniel and his father were to ride there on horseback. That was almost the only way of traveling in those days.

The next morning two horses were brought to the door. One was Judge Webster's horse, the other was a gentle nag, with a lady's sidesaddle on his back.

"Who is going to ride on that nag?" asked Daniel.

"Young Dan Webster," answered the judge.

"But I don't want a sidesaddle. I am not a lady."

"Neighbor Johnson is sending the nag to Exeter for the use of a lady who is to ride back with me. I accommodate him by taking charge of the animal, and he accommodates me by allowing you to ride on it."

"But won't it look rather funny for me to ride to Exeter on a lady's saddle?"

"If a lady can ride on it, perhaps Dan Webster can do as much."

And so they set out on their journey to Exeter. The judge rode in advance, and Daniel, sitting astride of the lady's saddle, followed behind.

It was, no doubt, a funny sight to see them riding thus along the muddy roads. None of the country people who stopped to gaze at them could have guessed that the dark-faced lad who rode so awkwardly would some day become one of the greatest men of the age.

It was thus that Daniel Webster made his first appearance among strangers.

At Exeter Academy

It was the first time that Daniel Webster had been so far from home. He was bashful and awkward. His clothes were of home-made stuff, and they were cut in the quaint style of the back-country districts.

He must have been a funny-looking fellow. No wonder that the boys laughed when they saw him going up to the principal to be examined for admission.

The principal of the academy at that time was Dr. Benjamin Abbott. He was a great scholar and a very dignified gentleman.

He looked down at the slender, black-eyed boy and asked:

"What is your age, sir?"

"Fourteen years," said Daniel.

"I will examine you first in reading. Take this Bible, and let me hear you read some of these verses."

He pointed to the twenty-second chapter of Saint Luke's Gospel.

The boy took the book and began to read. He had read this chapter a hundred times before. Indeed, there was no part of the Bible that was not familiar to him.

He read with a clearness and fervor which few men could equal.

The dignified principal was astonished. He stood as though spell-bound, listening to the rich, mellow tones of the bashful lad from among the hills.

In the case of most boys it was enough if he heard them read a verse or two. But he allowed Daniel Webster to read on until he had finished the chapter. Then he said:

"There is no need to examine you further. You are fully qualified to enter this academy."

Most of the boys at Exeter were gentlemen's sons. They dressed well, they had been taught fine manners, they had the speech of cultivated people.

They laughed at the awkward, new boy. They made fun of his homespun coat; they twitted him on account of his poverty; they annoyed him in a hundred ways.

Daniel felt hurt by this cruel treatment. He grieved bitterly over it in secret, but he did not resent it.

He studied hard and read much. He was soon at the head of all his classes. His schoolmates ceased laughing at him; for they saw that, with all his uncouth ways, he had more ability than any of them.

He had, as I have said, a wonderful memory. He had also a quick insight and sound judgment.

But he had had so little experience with the world, that he was not sure of his own powers. He knew that he was awkward; and this made him timid and bashful.

When it came his turn to declaim before the school, he had not the courage to do it. Long afterwards, when he had become the greatest orator of modern times, he told how hard this thing had been for him at Exeter:

"Many a piece did I commit to memory, and rehearse in my room over and over again. But when the day came, when the school collected, when my name was called and I saw all eyes turned upon my seat, I could not raise myself from it.

"Sometimes the masters frowned, sometimes they smiled. My tutor always pressed and entreated with the most winning kindness that I would venture only once; but I could not command sufficient resolution, and when the occasion was over I went home and wept tears of bitter mortification."

Daniel stayed nine months at Exeter. In those nine months he did as much as the other boys of his age could do in two years.

He mastered arithmetic, geography, grammar, and rhetoric. He also began the study of Latin. Besides this, he was a great reader of all kinds of books, and he added something every day to his general stock of knowledge.

His teachers did not oblige him to follow a graded course of study. They did not hold him back with the duller pupils of his class. They did not oblige him to wait until the end of the year before he could be promoted or could begin the study of a new subject.

But they encouraged him to do his best. As soon as he had finished one subject, he advanced to a more difficult one.

More than fifty years afterwards, Dr. Abbott declared that in all his long experience he had never known any one whose power of gaining knowledge was at all equal to that of the bashful country lad from the New Hampshire hills.

Judge Webster would have been glad to let Daniel stay at Exeter until he had finished the studies required at the academy. But he could not afford the expense.

If he should spend all his money to keep the boy at the academy, how could he afterwards find the means to send him to college where the expenses would be much greater?

So he thought it best to find a private teacher for the boy. This would be cheaper.

Getting Ready for College

One day in the early winter, Judge Webster asked Daniel to ride with him to Boscawen. Boscawen was a little town, six miles away, where they sometimes went for business or for pleasure.

Snow was on the ground. Father and son rode together in a little, old-fashioned sleigh; and as they rode, they talked about many things. Just as they were going up the last hill, Judge Webster said:

"Daniel, do you know the Rev. Samuel Wood, here in Boscawen?"

"I have heard of him," said Daniel. "He takes boys into his family, and gets them ready for college."

"Yes, and he does it cheap, too," said his father. "He charges only a dollar a week for board and tuition, fuel and lights and everything."

"But they say he is a fine teacher," said Daniel. "His boys never fail in the college examinations."

"That is what I have heard, too," answered his father. "And now, Dannie, I may as well tell you a secret. For the last six years I have been planning to have you take a course in Dartmouth College. I want you to stay with Dr. Wood this winter, and he will get you ready to enter. We might as well go and see him now."

This was the first time that Daniel had ever heard his father speak of sending him to college. His heart was so full that he could not say a word. But the tears came in his eyes as he looked up into the judge's stern, kind face.

He knew that if his father carried out this plan, it would cost a great deal of money; and if this money should be spent for him, then the rest of the family would have to deny themselves of many comforts which they might otherwise have.

"Oh, never mind that, Dan," said his brother Ezekiel. "We are never so happy as when we are doing something for you. And we know that you will do something for us, some time."

And so the boy spent the winter in Boscawen with Dr. Wood. He learned everything very easily, but he was not as close a student as he had been at Exeter.

He was very fond of sport. He liked to go fishing. And sometimes, when the weather was fine, his studies were sadly neglected.

There was a circulating library in Boscawen, and Daniel read every book that was in it. Sometimes he slighted his Latin for the sake of giving more time to such reading.

One of the books in the library was *Don Quixote*. Daniel thought it the most wonderful story in existence. He afterwards said:

"I began to read it, and it is literally true that I never closed my eyes until I had finished it, so great was the power of this extraordinary book on my imagination."

But it was so easy for the boy to learn, that he made very rapid progress in all his studies. In less than a year, Dr Wood declared that he was ready for college.

He was then fifteen years old. He had a pretty thorough knowledge of arithmetic; but he had never studied algebra or geometry. In Latin he had read four of Cicero's orations, and six books of Virgil's *Æneid*. He knew something of the elements of Greek grammar, and had read a portion of the Greek Testament.

Nowadays, a young man could hardly enter even a third-rate college without a better preparation than that. But colleges are much more thorough than they were a hundred years ago.

At Dartmouth College

Dartmouth College is at Hanover, New Hampshire. It is one of the oldest colleges in America and among its students have been many of the foremost men of New England.

It was in the fall of 1797, that Daniel Webster entered this college.

He was then a tall, slender youth, with high cheek bones and a swarthy skin.

The professors soon saw that he was no common lad. They said to one another, "This young Webster will one day be a greater man than any of us."

And young Webster was well-behaved and studious at college. He was as fond of sport as any of the students, but he never gave himself up to boyish pranks.

He was punctual and regular in all his classes. He was as great a reader as ever.

He could learn anything that he tried. No other young man had a broader knowledge of things than he.

And yet he did not make his mark as a student in the prescribed branches of study. He could not confine himself to the narrow routine of the college course.

He did not, as at Exeter, push his way quickly to the head of his class. He won no prizes.

"But he minded his own business," said one of the professors. "As steady as the sun, he pursued, with intense application, the great object for which he came to college."

Soon everybody began to appreciate his scholarship. Everybody admired him for his manliness and good common sense.

"He was looked upon as being so far in advance of any one else, that no other student of his class was ever spoken of as second to him."

He very soon lost that bashfulness which had troubled him so much at Exeter. It was no task now for him to stand up and declaim before the professors and students.

In a short time he became known as the best writer and speaker in the college. Indeed, he loved to speak; and the other students were always pleased to listen to him.

One of his classmates tells us how he prepared his speeches. He says: "It was Webster's custom to arrange his thoughts in his mind while he was in his room, or while he was walking alone. Then he would put them upon paper just before the exercise was to be called for.

"If he was to speak at two o'clock, he would often begin to write after dinner; and when the bell rang he would fold his paper, put it in his pocket, go in, and speak with great ease.

"In his movements he was slow and deliberate, except when his feelings were aroused. Then his whole soul would kindle into a flame."

In the year 1800, he was chosen to deliver the Fourth of July address to the students of the college and the citizens of the town. He was then eighteen years old.

The speech was a long one. It was full of the love of country. Its tone throughout was earnest and thoughtful.

But in its style it was overdone; it was full of pretentious expressions; it lacked the simplicity and good common sense that should mark all public addresses.

And yet, as the speech of so young a man, it was a very able effort. People said that it was the promise of much greater things. And they were right.

In the summer of 1801, Daniel graduated. But he took no honors. He was not even present at the Commencement.

His friends were grieved that he had not been chosen to deliver the valedictory address. Perhaps he also was disappointed. But the professors had thought best to give that honor to another student.

How Daniel Taught School

While Daniel Webster was taking his course in college, there was one thing that troubled him very much. It was the thought of his brother Ezekiel toiling at home on the farm.

He knew that Ezekiel had great abilities. He knew that he was not fond of the farm, but that he was anxious to become a lawyer.

This brother had given up all his dearest plans in order that Daniel might be favored; and Daniel knew that this was so.

Once, when Daniel was at home on a vacation, he said, "Zeke, this thing is all wrong. Father has mortgaged the farm for money to pay my expenses at school, and you are making a slave of yourself to pay off the mortgage. It isn't right for me to let you do this."

Ezekiel said, "Daniel, I am stronger than you are, and if one of us has to stay on the farm, of course I am the one."

"But I want you to go to college," said Daniel. "An education will do you as much good as me."

"I doubt it," said Ezekiel; "and yet, if father was only able to send us both, I think that we might pay him back some time."

"I will see father about it this very day," said Daniel.

He did see him.

"I told my father," said Daniel, afterwards, "that I was unhappy at my brother's prospects. For myself, I saw my way to knowledge, respectability, and self-protection. But as to Ezekiel, all looked the other way. I said that I would keep school, and get along as well as I could, be more than four years in getting through college, if necessary, provided he also could be sent to study."

The matter was referred to Daniel's mother, and she and his father talked it over together. They knew that it would take all the property they had to educate both the boys. They knew that they would have to do without many comforts, and that they would have a hard struggle to make a living while the boys were studying.

But the mother said, "I will trust the boys." And it was settled that Ezekiel, too, should have a chance to make his mark in the world.

He was now a grown-up man. He was tall and strong and ambitious. He entered college the very year that Daniel graduated.

As for Daniel, he was now ready to choose a profession. What should it be?

His father wanted him to become a lawyer. And so, to please his parents, he went home and began to read law in the office of a Mr. Thompson, in the little village of Salisbury, which adjoined his father's farm.

The summer passed by. It was very pleasant to have nothing to do but to read. And when the young man grew tired of reading, he could go out fishing, or could spend a day in hunting among the New Hampshire hills.

It is safe to say that he did not learn very much law during that summer.

But there was not a day that he did not think about his brother. Ezekiel had done much to help him through college, and now ought he not to help Ezekiel?

But what could he do?

He had a good education, and his first thought was that he might teach school, and thus earn a little money for Ezekiel.

The people of Fryeburg, in Maine, wanted him to take charge of the academy in their little town. And so, early in the fall, he decided to take up with their offer.

He was to have three hundred and fifty dollars for the year's work, and that would help Ezekiel a great deal.

He bade good-bye to Mr. Thompson and his little law office, and made ready to go to his new field of labor. There were no railroads at that time, and a journey of even a few miles was a great undertaking.

Daniel had bought a horse for twenty-four dollars. In one end of an old-fashioned pair of saddlebags he put his Sunday clothes, and in the other he packed his books.

He laid the saddlebags upon the horse, then he mounted and rode off over the hills toward Fryeburg, sixty miles away.

He was not yet quite twenty years old. He was very slender, and nearly six feet in height. His face was thin and dark. His eyes were black and bright and penetrating—no person who once saw them could ever forget them.

Young as he was, he was very successful as a teacher during that year which he spent at Fryeburg. The trustees of the academy were so highly pleased that they wanted him to stay a second year. They promised to raise his salary to five or six hundred dollars, and to give him a house and a piece of land.

He was greatly tempted to give up all further thoughts of becoming a lawyer.

"What shall I do?" he said to himself. "Shall I say, 'Yes, gentlemen,' and sit down here to spend my days in a kind of comfortable privacy?"

But his father was anxious that he should return to the study of the law. And so he was not long in making up his mind.

In a letter to one of his friends he said: "I shall make one more trial of the law in the ensuing autumn.

"If I prosecute the profession, I pray God to fortify me against its temptations. To be honest, to be capable, to be faithful to my client and my conscience."

Early the next September, he was again in Mr. Thompson's little law office. All the money that he had saved, while at Fryeburg, was spent to help Ezekiel through college.

Daniel Goes to Boston

For a year and a half, young Daniel Webster stayed in the office of Mr. Thompson. He had now fully made up his mind as to what profession he would follow; and so he was a much better student than he had been before.

He read many law books with care. He read *Hume's History of England*, and spent a good deal of time with the Latin classics.

"At this period of my life," he afterwards said, "I passed a great deal of time alone.

"My amusements were fishing and shooting and riding, and all these were without a companion. I loved this solitude then, and have loved it ever since, and love it still."

The Webster family were still very poor. Judge Webster was now too old to do much work of any kind. The farm had been mortgaged for all that it was worth. It was hard to find money enough to keep Daniel at his law studies and Ezekiel in college.

At last it became necessary for one of the young men to do something that would help matters along. Ezekiel decided that he would leave college for a time and try to earn enough money to meet the present needs of the family. Through some of his friends he obtained a small private school in Boston.

There were very few pupils in Ezekiel Webster's school. But there were so many branches to be taught that he could not find time to hear all the recitations. So, at last, he sent word to Daniel to come down and help him. If Daniel would teach an hour and a half each day, he should have enough money to pay his board.

Daniel was pleased with the offer. He had long wanted to study law in Boston, and here was his opportunity. And so, early in March, 1804, he joined his brother in that city, and was soon doing what he could to help him in his little school.

There was in Boston, at that time, a famous lawyer whose name was Christopher Gore. While Daniel Webster was wondering how he could best carry on his studies in the city, he heard that Mr. Gore had no clerk in his office.

"How I should like to read law with Mr. Gore!" he said to Ezekiel.

"Yes," said Ezekiel. "You could not want a better tutor."

"I mean to see him to-day and apply for a place in his office," said Daniel.

It was with many misgivings that the young man went into the presence of the great lawyer. We will let him tell the story in his own words:

"I was from the country, I said;—had studied law for two years; had come to Boston to study a year more; had heard that he had no clerk; thought it possible he would receive one.

"I told him that I came to Boston to work, not to play; was most desirous, on all accounts, to be his pupil; and all I ventured to ask at present was, that he would keep a place for me in his office, till I could write to New Hampshire for proper letters showing me worthy of it."

Mr. Gore listened to this speech very kindly, and then bade Daniel be seated while he should have a short talk with him.

When at last the young man rose to go, Mr. Gore said: "My young friend, you look as if you might be trusted. You say you came to study and not to waste time. I will take you at your word. You may as well hang up your hat at once."

And this was the beginning of Daniel Webster's career in Boston.

He must have done well in Mr. Gore's office; for, in a few months, he was admitted to the practice of law in the Court of Common Pleas in Boston.

It was at some time during this same winter that Daniel was offered the position of clerk in the County Court at home. His father, as you will remember, was one of the judges in this court, and he was very much delighted at the thought that his son would be with him.

The salary would be about fifteen hundred dollars a year—and that was a great sum to Daniel as well as to his father. The mortgage on the farm could be paid off; Ezekiel could finish his course in college; and life would be made easier for them all.

At first Daniel was as highly pleased as his father. But after he had talked with Mr. Gore, he decided not to accept the offered position.

"Your prospects as a lawyer," said Mr. Gore, "are good enough to encourage you to go on. Go on, and finish your studies. You are poor enough, but there are greater evils than poverty. Live on no man's favor. Pursue your profession; make yourself useful to your friends and a little formidable to your enemies, and you have nothing to fear."

A few days after that, Daniel paid a visit to his father. The judge received him very kindly, but he was greatly disappointed when the young man told him that he had made up his mind not to take the place.

With his deep-set, flashing eyes, he looked at his son for a moment as though in anger. Then he said, very slowly:

"Well, my son, your mother has always said that you would come to something or nothing—she was not sure which. I think you are now about settling that doubt for her."

A few weeks after this, Daniel, as I have already told you, was admitted to the bar in Boston. But he did not think it best to begin his practice there.

He knew how anxious his father was that he should be near him. He wanted to do all that he could to cheer and comfort the declining years of the noble man who had sacrificed everything for him. And so, in the spring of 1805, he settled in the town of Boscawen, six miles from home, and put up at his office door this sign:

> D. WEBSTER, *Attorney*

Lawyer and Congressman

When Daniel Webster had been in Boscawen nearly two years, his father died. It was then decided that Ezekiel should come and take charge of the home farm, and care for their mother.

Ezekiel had not yet graduated from college, but he had read law and was hoping to be admitted to the bar. He was a man of much natural ability, and many people believed that he would some day become a very famous lawyer.

And so, in the autumn of 1807, Daniel gave up to his brother the law business which he had in Boscawen, and removed to the city of Portsmouth.

He was now twenty-five years old. In Portsmouth he would find plenty of work to do; it would be the very kind of work that he liked. He was now well started on the road towards greatness.

The very next year, he was married to Miss Grace Fletcher, the daughter of a minister in Hopkinton. The happy couple began housekeeping in a small, modest, wooden house, in Portsmouth; and there they lived, very plainly and without pretension, for several years.

Mr. Webster's office was "a common, ordinary-looking room, with less furniture and more books than common. He had a small inner room, opening from the larger, rather an unusual thing."

It was not long until the name of Daniel Webster was known all over New Hampshire. Those who were acquainted with him said that he was the smartest young lawyer in Portsmouth. They said that if he kept on in the way that he had started, there were great things in store for him.

The country people told wonderful stories about him. They said that he was as black as a coal—but of course they had never seen him. They believed that he could gain any case in court that he chose to manage—and in this they were about right.

There was another great lawyer in Portsmouth. His name was Jeremiah Mason, and he was much older than Mr. Webster. Indeed, he was already a famous man when Daniel first began the practice of law.

The young lawyer and the older one soon became warm friends; and yet they were often opposed to each other in the courts. Daniel was always obliged to do his best when Mr. Mason was against him. This caused him to be very careful. It no doubt made him become a better lawyer than he otherwise would have been.

DANIEL WEBSTER

While Webster was thus quietly practicing law in New Hampshire, trouble was brewing between the United States and England. The English were doing much to hinder American merchants from trading with foreign countries.

They claimed the right to search American vessels for seamen who had deserted from the British service. And it is said that American sailors were often dragged from their own vessels and forced to serve on board the English ships.

Matters kept getting worse and worse for several years. At last, in June, 1812, the United States declared war against England.

Daniel Webster was opposed to this war, and he made several speeches against it. He said that, although we had doubtless suffered many wrongs, there was more cause for war with France than with England. And then, the United States had no navy, and hence was not ready to go to war with any nation.

Webster's influence in New Hampshire was so great that he persuaded many of the people of that state to think just as he thought on this subject. They nominated him as their representative in Congress; and when the time came, they elected him.

It was on the 24th of May, 1813, that he first took his seat in Congress. He was then thirty-one years old.

In that same Congress there were two other young men who afterwards made their names famous in the history of their country. One was Henry Clay, of

Kentucky. The other was John C. Calhoun, of South Carolina. Both were a little older than Webster; both had already made some mark in public life; and both were in favor of the war.

During his first year in Congress, Mr. Webster made some stirring speeches in support of his own opinions. In this way, as well by his skill in debate, he made himself known as a young man of more than common ability and promise.

Chief Justice Marshall, who was then at the head of the Supreme Court of the United States, said of him: "I have never seen a man of whose intellect I had a higher opinion."

In 1814, the war that had been going on so long came to an end. But now there were other subjects which claimed Mr. Webster's attention in Congress.

Then, as now, there were important questions regarding the money of the nation; and upon these questions there was great difference of opinion. Daniel Webster's speeches, in favor of a sound currency, did much to maintain the national credit and to save the country from bankruptcy.

The people of New Hampshire were so well pleased with the record which he made in Congress that, when his first term expired, they reëlected him for a second.

The Dartmouth College Case

In 1816, before his second term in Congress had expired, Daniel Webster removed with his family to Boston. He had lived in Portsmouth nine years, and he now felt that he needed a wider field for the exercise of his talents.

He was now no longer the slender, delicate person that he had been in his boyhood and youth. He was a man of noble mien—a sturdy, dignified personage, who bore the marks of greatness upon him. People said, "When Daniel Webster walked the streets of Boston, he made the buildings look small."

As soon as his term in Congress had expired, he began the practice of law in Boston.

For nearly seven years he devoted himself strictly to his profession. Of course, he at once took his place as the leading lawyer of New England. Indeed, he soon became known as the ablest counsellor and advocate in America.

The best business of the country now came to him. His income was very large, amounting to more than $20,000 a year.

And during this time there was no harder worker than he. In fact, his natural genius could have done but little for him, had it not been for his untiring industry.

One of his first great victories in law was that which is known as the Dartmouth College case. The lawmakers of New Hampshire had attempted to pass a law to alter the charter of the college. By doing this they would endanger the usefulness and prosperity of that great school, in order to favor the selfish projects of its enemies.

Daniel Webster undertook to defend the college. The speech which he made before the Supreme Court of the United States was a masterly effort.

"Sir," he said, "you may destroy this little institution—it is weak, it is in your hands. I know it is one of the lesser lights in the literary horizon of our country. You may put it out.

"But if you do so, you must carry through your work! You must extinguish, one after another, all those greater lights of science which, for more than a century, have thrown their light over our land!"

He won the case; and this, more than anything else, helped to gain for him the reputation of being the ablest lawyer in the United States.

Webster's Great Orations

In 1820, when he was thirty-eight years old, Daniel Webster was chosen to deliver an oration at a great meeting of New Englanders at Plymouth, Massachusetts.

DANIEL WEBSTER

Plymouth is the place where the Pilgrims landed in 1620. Just two hundred years had passed since that time, and this meeting was to celebrate the memory of the brave men and women who had risked so much to found new homes in what was then a bleak wilderness.

The speech which Mr. Webster delivered was one of the greatest ever heard in America. It placed him at once at the head of American orators.

John Adams, the second president of the United States, was then living, a very old man. He said, "This oration will be read five hundred years hence with as much rapture as it was heard. It ought to be read at the end of every century, and, indeed, at the end of every year, forever and ever."

But this was only the first of many great addresses by Mr. Webster. In 1825, he delivered an oration at the laying of the corner stone of the Bunker Hill monument. Eighteen years later, when that monument was finished, he delivered another. Many of Mr. Webster's admirers think that these two orations are his masterpieces.

On July 4th, 1826, the United States had been independent just fifty years. On that day there passed away two of the greatest men of the country—John Adams and Thomas Jefferson.

Both were ex-Presidents, and both had been leaders in the councils of the nation. It was in memory of these two patriots that Daniel Webster was called to deliver an oration in Faneuil Hall, Boston.

No other funeral oration has ever been delivered in any age or country that was equal to this in eloquence. Like all his other discourses, it was full of patriotic feeling.

"This lovely land," he said, "this glorious liberty, these benign institutions, the dear purchase of our fathers, are ours; ours to enjoy, ours to preserve, ours to transmit. Generations past and generations to come hold us responsible for this sacred trust.

"Our fathers, from behind, admonish us with their anxious, paternal voices; posterity calls out to us from the bosom of the future; the world turns hither its solicitous eyes; all, all conjure us to act wisely and faithfully in the relation which we sustain."

Most of his other great speeches were delivered in Congress, and are, therefore, political in tone and subject.

Great as Daniel Webster was in politics and in law, it is as an orator and patriot that his name will be longest remembered.

Mr. Webster in the Senate

When Daniel Webster was forty years old, the people of Boston elected him to represent them in Congress. They were so well pleased with all that he did while there, that they reëlected him twice.

In June, 1827, the legislature of Massachusetts chose him to be United States senator for a term of six years. He was at that time the most famous man in Massachusetts, and his name was known and honored in every state of the Union.

After that he was reëlected to the same place again and again; and for more than twenty years he continued to be the distinguished senator from Massachusetts.

I cannot now tell you of all his public services during the long period that he sat in Congress. Indeed, there are some things that you would find hard to understand until you have learned more about the history of our country. But you will by-and-by read of them in the larger books which you will study at school; and, no doubt, you will also read some of his great addresses and orations.

It was in 1830 that he delivered the most famous of all his speeches in the senate chamber of the United States. This speech is commonly called, "The Reply to Hayne."

I shall not here try to explain the purport of Mr. Hayne's speeches—for there were two of them. I shall not try to describe the circumstances which led Mr. Webster to make his famous reply to them.

But I will quote Mr. Webster's closing sentences. Forty years ago the schoolboys all over the country were accustomed to memorize and declaim these patriotic utterances.

"When my eyes shall be turned to behold, for the last time, the sun in heaven, may I not see him shining on the broken and dishonored fragments of a once glorious Union; on states dissevered, discordant, belligerent, on a land rent with civil feuds, or drenched, it may be, in fraternal blood!

"Let their last feeble and lingering glance rather behold the gorgeous ensign of the republic, now known and honored throughout the earth, still high advanced, its arms and trophies streaming in their original luster, not a stripe erased or polluted, not a single star obscured, bearing for its motto no such miserable interrogatory, 'What is all this worth?' nor those other words of delusion and folly, 'Liberty first and Union afterwards;' but everywhere, spread all over in characters of living light, blazing on all its folds, as they float over the land, and in every wind under the whole heavens, that other sentiment, dear to every American heart—Liberty and Union, now and forever, one and inseparable!"

In 1841, Daniel Webster resigned his seat in the senate. He did this in order to become secretary of state in the cabinet of the newly elected President, William Henry Harrison.

But President Harrison died on the 5th of April, after having held his office just one month; and his place was taken by the vice-president, John Tyler. Mr. Webster now felt that his position in the cabinet would not be a pleasant one; but he continued to hold it for nearly two years.

His most important act as secretary of state was to conclude a treaty with England which fixed the northeastern boundary of the United States. This treaty is known in history as the Ashburton Treaty.

In 1843, Mr. Webster resigned his place in President Tyler's cabinet. But he was not allowed to remain long in private life. Two years later he was again elected to the United States senate.

About this time, Texas was annexed to the United States. But Mr. Webster did not favor this, for he believed that such an act was contrary to the Constitution of our country.

He did all that he could to keep our government from making war upon Mexico. But after this war had been begun, he was a firm friend of the soldiers who took part in it, and he did much to provide for their safety and comfort.

Among these soldiers was Edward, the second son of Daniel Webster. He became a major in the main division of the army, and died in the City of Mexico.

Mr. Webster in Private Life

Let us now go back a little way in our story, and learn something about Mr. Webster's home and private life.

The Mansion at Marshfield.
THE LIBRARY.
DANIEL WEBSTER.
The Tomb.

In 1831, Mr. Webster bought a large farm at Marshfield, in the southeastern part of Massachusetts, not far from the sea.

He spent a great deal of money in improving this farm; and in the end it was as fine a country seat as one might see anywhere in New England.

When he became tired with the many cares of his busy life, Mr. Webster could always find rest and quiet days at Marshfield. He liked to dress himself as a farmer, and stroll about the fields looking at the cattle and at the growing crops.

"I had rather be here than in the senate," he would say.

But his life was clouded with many sorrows. Long before going to Marshfield, his two eldest children were laid in the grave. Their mother followed them just one year before Mr. Webster's first entry into the United States senate.

In 1829, his brother Ezekiel died suddenly while speaking in court at Concord. Ezekiel had never cared much for politics, but as a lawyer in his native state, he had won many honors. His death came as a great shock to everybody that knew him. To his brother it brought overwhelming sorrow.

When Daniel Webster was nearly forty-eight years old, he married a second wife. She was the daughter of a New York merchant, and her name was Caroline Bayard Le Roy. She did much to lighten the disappointments of his later life, and they lived together happily for more than twenty years.

In 1839, Mr. and Mrs. Webster made a short visit to England. The fame of the great orator had gone before him, and he was everywhere received with honor. The greatest men of the time were proud to meet him.

Henry Hallam, the historian, wrote of him: "Mr. Webster approaches as nearly to the *beau ideal* of a republican senator as any man that I have ever seen in the course of my life."

Even the Queen invited him to dine with her; and she was much pleased with his dignified ways and noble bearing.

And, indeed, his appearance was such as to win the respect of all who saw him. When he walked the streets of London, people would stop and wonder who the noble stranger was; and workingmen whispered to one another: "There goes a king!"

The Last Years

Many people believed that Daniel Webster would finally be elected President of the United States. And, indeed, there was no man in all this country who was better fitted for that high position than he.

But it so happened that inferior men, who were willing to stoop to the tricks of politics, always stepped in before him.

In the meanwhile the question of slavery was becoming, every day, more and more important. It was the one subject which claimed everybody's attention.

Should slavery be allowed in the territories?

There was great excitement all over the country. There were many hot debates in Congress. It seemed as though the Union would be destroyed.

At last, the wiser and cooler-headed leaders in Congress said, "Let each side give up a little to the other. Let us have a compromise."

On the 7th of March, 1850, Mr. Webster delivered a speech before the senate. It was a speech in favor of compromise, in favor of conciliation.

He thought that this was the only way to preserve the Union. And he was willing to sacrifice everything for the Constitution and the Union.

He declared that all the ends he aimed at were for his country's good.

"I speak to-day for the preservation of the Union," he said. "Hear me for my cause! I speak to-day out of a solicitous and anxious heart, for the restoration to the country of that quiet and harmony, which make the blessings of this Union so rich and so dear to us all."

He then went on to defend the law known as the Fugitive Slave Law. He declared that this law was in accordance with the Constitution, and hence it should be enforced according to its true meaning.

The speech was a great disappointment to his friends. They said that he had deserted them; that he had gone over to their enemies; that he was no longer a champion of freedom, but of slavery.

Those who had been his warmest supporters, now turned against him.

A few months after this, President Taylor died. The vice-president, Millard Fillmore, then became president. Mr. Fillmore was in sympathy with Daniel Webster, and soon gave him a seat in his cabinet as secretary of state.

This was the second time that Mr. Webster had been called to fill this high and honorable position. But, under President Fillmore, he did no very great or important thing.

He was still the leading man in the Whig party; and he hoped, in 1852, to be nominated for the presidency. But in this he was again disappointed.

He was now an old man. He had had great successes in life; but he felt that he had failed at the end of the race. His health was giving way. He went home to Marshfield for the quiet and rest which he so much needed.

In May, that same year, he was thrown from his carriage and severely hurt. From this hurt he never recovered. He offered to resign his seat in the cabinet, but Mr. Fillmore would not listen to this.

In September he became very feeble, and his friends knew that the end was near. On the 24th of

October, 1852, he died. He was nearly seventy-one years old.

In every part of the land his death was sincerely mourned. Both friends and enemies felt that a great man had fallen. They felt that this country had lost its leading statesman, its noblest patriot, its worthiest citizen.

Rufus Choate, who had succeeded him as the foremost lawyer in New England, delivered a great oration upon his life and character. He said:

"Look in how manly a sort, in how high a moral tone, Mr. Webster uniformly dealt with the mind of his country.

"Where do you find him flattering his countrymen, indirectly or directly, for a vote? On what did he ever place himself but good counsels and useful service?

"Who ever heard that voice cheering the people on to rapacity, to injustice, to a vain and guilty glory?

"How anxiously, rather, did he prefer to teach, that by all possible acquired sobriety of mind, by asking reverently of the past, by obedience to the law, by habits of patient labor, by the cultivation of the mind, by the fear and worship of God, we educate ourselves for the future that is revealing."

THE STORY OF ABRAHAM LINCOLN

A. Lincoln.

THE STORY OF ABRAHAM LINCOLN

The Kentucky Home

Not far from Hodgensville, in Kentucky, there once lived a man whose name was Thomas Lincoln. This man had built for himself a little log cabin by the side of a brook, where there was an ever-flowing spring of water.

There was but one room in this cabin. On the side next to the brook there was a low doorway; and at one end there was a large fireplace, built of rough stones and clay.

The chimney was very broad at the bottom and narrow at the top. It was made of clay, with flat stones and slender sticks laid around the outside to keep it from falling apart.

In the wall, on one side of the fireplace, there was a square hole for a window. But there was no glass in this window. In the summer it was left open all the time. In cold weather a deerskin, or a piece of coarse cloth, was hung over it to keep out the wind and the snow.

At night, or on stormy days, the skin of a bear was hung across the doorway; for there was no door on hinges to be opened and shut.

There was no ceiling to the room. But the inmates of the cabin, by looking up, could see the bare rafters and the rough roof-boards, which Mr. Lincoln himself had split and hewn.

There was no floor, but only the bare ground that had been smoothed and beaten until it was as level and hard as pavement.

For chairs there were only blocks of wood and a rude bench on one side of the fireplace. The bed was a little platform of poles, on which were spread the furry skins of wild animals, and a patchwork quilt of homespun goods.

In this poor cabin, on the 12th of February, 1809, a baby boy was born. There was already one child in the family—a girl, two years old, whose name was Sarah.

The little boy grew and became strong like other babies, and his parents named him Abraham, after his grandfather, who had been killed by the Indians many years before.

When he was old enough to run about, he liked to play under the trees by the cabin door. Sometimes he would go with his little sister into the woods and watch the birds and the squirrels.

He had no playmates. He did not know the meaning of toys or playthings. But he was a happy child and had many pleasant ways.

Thomas Lincoln, the father, was a kind-hearted man, very strong and brave. Sometimes he would take the child on his knee and tell him strange, true stories of the great forest, and of the Indians and the fierce beasts that roamed among the woods and hills.

For Thomas Lincoln had always lived on the wild frontier; and he would rather hunt deer and other game in the forest than do anything else. Perhaps this is why he was so poor. Perhaps this is why he was content to live in the little log cabin with so few of the comforts of life.

But Nancy Lincoln, the young mother, did not complain. She, too, had grown up among the rude scenes of the backwoods. She had never known better things.

And yet she was by nature refined and gentle; and people who knew her said that she was very handsome. She was a model housekeeper, too; and her poor log cabin was the neatest and best-kept house in all that neighborhood.

No woman could be busier than she. She knew how to spin and weave, and she made all the clothing for her family.

She knew how to wield the ax and the hoe; and she could work on the farm or in the garden when her help was needed.

She had also learned how to shoot with a rifle; and she could bring down a deer or other wild game with as much ease as could her husband. And when the game was brought home, she could dress it, she could cook the flesh for food, and of the skins she could make clothing for her husband and children.

There was still another thing that she could do—she could read; and she read all the books that she could get hold of. She taught her husband the letters of the alphabet; and she showed him how to write his name. For Thomas Lincoln had never gone to school, and he had never learned how to read.

As soon as little Abraham Lincoln was old enough to understand, his mother read stories to him from the Bible. Then, while he was still very young, she taught him to read the stories for himself.

The neighbors thought it a wonderful thing that so small a boy could read. There were very few of them who could do as much. Few of them thought it of any great use to learn how to read.

There were no schoolhouses in that part of Kentucky in those days, and of course there were no public schools.

One winter a traveling schoolmaster came that way. He got leave to use a cabin not far from Mr. Lincoln's, and gave notice that he would teach school for two or three weeks. The people were too poor to pay him for teaching longer.

The name of this schoolmaster was Zachariah Riney.

The young people for miles around flocked to the school. Most of them were big boys and girls, and a few were grown up young men. The only little child was Abraham Lincoln, and he was not yet five years old.

There was only one book studied at that school, and it was a spelling book. It had some easy reading lessons at the end, but these were not to be read until after every word in the book had been spelled.

You can imagine how the big boys and girls felt when Abraham Lincoln proved that he could spell and read better than any of them.

Work and Sorrow

In the autumn, just after Abraham Lincoln was eight years old, his parents left their Kentucky home and moved to Spencer county, in Indiana.

It was not yet a year since Indiana had become a state. Land could be bought very cheap, and Mr. Lincoln thought that he could make a good living there for his family. He had heard also that game was plentiful in the Indiana woods.

It was not more than seventy or eighty miles from the old home to the new. But it seemed very far, indeed, and it was a good many days before the travelers reached their journey's end. Over a part of the way there was no road, and the movers had to cut a path for themselves through the thick woods.

The boy, Abraham, was tall and very strong for his age. He already knew how to handle an ax, and few men could shoot with a rifle better than he. He was his father's helper in all kinds of work.

It was in November when the family came to the place which was to be their future home. Winter was near at hand. There was no house, nor shelter of any kind. What would become of the patient, tired mother, and the gentle little sister, who had borne themselves so bravely during the long, hard journey?

No sooner had the horses been loosed from the wagon than Abraham and his father were at work with their axes. In a short time they had built what they called a "camp."

This camp was but a rude shed, made of poles and thatched with leaves and branches. It was enclosed on three sides, so that the chill winds or the driving rains from the north and west could not enter. The fourth side was left open, and in front of it a fire was built.

This fire was kept burning all the time. It warmed the interior of the camp. A big iron kettle was hung over it by means of a chain and pole, and in this kettle the fat bacon, the venison, the beans, and the corn were boiled for the family's dinner and supper. In the hot ashes the good mother baked luscious "corn dodgers," and sometimes, perhaps, a few potatoes.

In one end of the camp were the few cooking utensils and little articles of furniture which even the poorest house cannot do without. The rest of the space was the family sitting room and bedroom. The floor was covered with leaves, and on these were spread the furry skins of deer and bears, and other animals.

It was in this camp that the family spent their first winter in Indiana. How very cold and dreary that winter must have been! Think of the stormy nights, of the shrieking wind, of the snow and the sleet and the bitter frost! It is not much wonder if, before the spring months came, the mother's strength began to fail.

But it was a busy winter for Thomas Lincoln. Every day his ax was heard in the woods. He was clearing the ground, so that in the spring it might be planted with corn and vegetables.

He was hewing logs for his new house; for he had made up his mind, now, to have something better than a cabin.

The woods were full of wild animals. It was easy for Abraham and his father to kill plenty of game, and thus keep the family supplied with fresh meat.

And Abraham, with chopping and hewing and hunting and trapping, was very busy for a little boy. He had but little time to play; and, since he had no playmates, we cannot know whether he even wanted to play.

With his mother, he read over and over the Bible stories which both of them loved so well. And, during the cold, stormy days, when he could not leave the camp, his mother taught him how to write.

In the spring the new house was raised. It was only a hewed log house, with one room below and a loft above. But it was so much better than the old cabin in Kentucky that it seemed like a palace.

The family had become so tired of living in the "camp," that they moved into the new house before the floor was laid, or any door hung at the doorway.

Then came the plowing and the planting and the hoeing. Everybody was busy from daylight to dark. There were so many trees and stumps that there was but little room for the corn to grow.

The summer passed, and autumn came. Then the poor mother's strength gave out. She could no longer go about her household duties. She had to depend more and more upon the help that her children could give her.

At length she became too feeble to leave her bed. She called her boy to her side. She put her arms about him and said: "Abraham, I am going away from you, and you will never see me again. I know that you will always be good and kind to your sister and father. Try to live as I have taught you, and to love your heavenly Father."

On the 5th of October she fell asleep, never to wake again.

Under a big sycamore tree, half a mile from the house, the neighbors dug the grave for the mother of Abraham Lincoln. And there they buried her in silence and great sorrow.

There was no minister there to conduct religious services. In all that new country there was no church; and no holy man could be found to speak words of comfort and hope to the grieving ones around the grave.

But the boy, Abraham, remembered a traveling preacher, whom they had known in Kentucky. The name of this preacher was David Elkin. If he would only come!

And so, after all was over, the lad sat down and wrote a letter to David Elkin. He was only a child nine years old, but he believed that the good man would remember his poor mother, and come.

It was no easy task to write a letter. Paper and ink were not things of common use, as they are with us. A pen had to be made from the quill of a goose.

But at last the letter was finished and sent away. How it was carried I do not know; for the mails were few and far between in those days, and postage was very high. It is more than likely that some friend, who was going into Kentucky, undertook to have it finally handed to the good preacher.

Months passed. The leaves were again on the trees. The wild flowers were blossoming in the woods. At last the preacher came.

He had ridden a hundred miles on horseback; he had forded rivers, and traveled through pathless woods; he had dared the dangers of the wild forest: all in answer to the lad's beseeching letter.

He had no hope of reward, save that which is given to every man who does his duty. He did not know that there would come a time when the greatest preachers in the world would envy him his sad task.

And now the friends and neighbors gathered again under the great sycamore tree. The funeral sermon was preached. Hymns were sung. A prayer was offered. Words of comfort and sympathy were spoken.

From that time forward the mind of Abraham Lincoln was filled with a high and noble purpose. In his earliest childhood his mother had taught him to love truth and justice, to be honest and upright among men, and to reverence God. These lessons he never forgot.

Long afterward, when he was known as a very great man, he said: "All that I am, or hope to be, I owe to my angel mother."

The New Mother

The log house, which Abraham Lincoln called his home, was now more lonely and cheerless than before. The sunlight of his mother's presence had gone out of it forever.

His sister Sarah, twelve years old, was the housekeeper and cook. His father had not yet found time to lay a floor in the house, or to hang a door. There were great crevices between the logs, through which the wind and the rain drifted on every stormy day. There was not much comfort in such a house.

But the lad was never idle. In the long winter days, when there was no work to be done, he spent the time in reading or in trying to improve his writing.

ABRAHAM LINCOLN

There were very few books in the cabins of that backwoods settlement. But if Abraham Lincoln heard of one, he could not rest till he had borrowed it and read it.

Another summer passed, and then another winter. Then, one day, Mr. Lincoln went on a visit to Kentucky, leaving his two children and their cousin, Dennis Hanks, at home to care for the house and the farm.

I do not know how long he stayed away, but it could not have been many weeks. One evening, the children were surprised to see a four-horse wagon draw up before the door.

Their father was in the wagon; and by his side was a kind-faced woman; and, sitting on the straw at the bottom of the wagon-bed, there were three well-dressed children—two girls and a boy.

And there were some grand things in the wagon, too. There were six split-bottomed chairs, a bureau with drawers, a wooden chest, and a feather bed. All these things were very wonderful to the lad and lassie who had never known the use of such luxuries.

"Abraham and Sarah," said Mr. Lincoln, as he leaped from the wagon, "I have brought you a new mother and a new brother and two new sisters."

The new mother greeted them very kindly, and, no doubt, looked with gentle pity upon them. They were barefooted; their scant clothing was little more than rags and tatters; they did not look much like her own happy children, whom she had cared for so well.

And now it was not long until a great change was made in the Lincoln home. A floor was laid, a door was hung, a window was made, the crevices between the logs were daubed with clay.

The house was furnished in fine style, with the chairs and the bureau and the feather bed. The kind, new mother brought sunshine and hope into the place that had once been so cheerless.

With the young lad, Dennis Hanks, there were now six children in the family. But all were treated with the same kindness; all had the same motherly care. And so, in the midst of much hard work, there were many pleasant days for them all.

School and Books

Not very long after this, the people of the neighborhood made up their minds that they must have a schoolhouse. And so, one day after harvest, the men met together and chopped down trees, and built a little low-roofed log cabin to serve for that purpose.

If you could see that cabin you would think it a queer kind of schoolhouse. There was no floor. There was only one window, and in it were strips of greased paper pasted across, instead of glass. There were no desks, but only rough benches made of logs split in

ABRAHAM LINCOLN

halves. In one end of the room was a huge fireplace; at the other end was the low doorway.

The first teacher was a man whose name was Azel Dorsey. The term of school was very short; for the settlers could not afford to pay him much. It was in midwinter, for then there was no work for the big boys to do at home.

And the big boys, as well as the girls and the smaller boys, for miles around, came in to learn what they could from Azel Dorsey. The most of the children studied only spelling; but some of the larger ones learned reading and writing and arithmetic.

There were not very many scholars, for the houses in that new settlement were few and far apart. School began at an early hour in the morning, and did not close until the sun was down.

Just how Abraham Lincoln stood in his classes I do not know; but I must believe that he studied hard and did everything as well as he could. In the arithmetic which he used, he wrote these lines:

> "Abraham Lincoln,
> His hand and pen,
> He will be good,
> But God knows when."

In a few weeks, Azel Dorsey's school came to a close; and Abraham Lincoln was again as busy as ever about his father's farm. After that he attended school only two or three short terms. If all his school days were put together they would not make a twelve-month.

But he kept on reading and studying at home. His stepmother said of him: "He read everything he could lay his hands on. When he came across a passage that struck him, he would write it down on boards, if he had no paper, and keep it until he had got paper. Then he would copy it, look at it, commit it to memory, and repeat it."

Among the books that he read were the Bible, the *Pilgrim's Progress*, and the poems of Robert Burns. One day he walked a long distance to borrow a book of a farmer. This book was Weems's *Life of Washington*. He read as much as he could while walking home.

By that time it was dark, and so he sat down by the chimney and read by fire light until bedtime. Then he took the book to bed with him in the loft, and read by the light of a tallow candle.

In an hour the candle burned out. He laid the book in a crevice between two of the logs of the cabin, so that he might begin reading again as soon as it was daylight.

But in the night a storm came up. The rain was blown in, and the book was wet through and through.

In the morning, when Abraham awoke, he saw what had happened. He dried the leaves as well as he could, and then finished reading the book.

As soon as he had eaten his breakfast, he hurried to carry the book to its owner. He explained how the accident had happened.

"Mr. Crawford," he said, "I am willing to pay you for the book. I have no money; but, if you will let me, I will work for you until I have made its price."

Mr. Crawford thought that the book was worth seventy-five cents, and that Abraham's work would be worth about twenty-five cents a day. And so the lad helped the farmer gather corn for three days, and thus became the owner of the delightful book.

He read the story of Washington many times over. He carried the book with him to the field, and read it while he was following the plow.

From that time, Washington was the one great hero whom he admired. Why could not he model his own life after that of Washington? Why could not he also be a doer of great things for his country?

Life in the Backwoods

Abraham Lincoln now set to work with a will to educate himself. His father thought that he did not need to learn anything more. He did not see that there was any good in book-learning. If a man could read and write and cipher, what more was needed?

But the good stepmother thought differently; and when another short term of school began in the little log school-house, all six of the children from the Lincoln cabin were among the scholars.

In a few weeks, however, the school had closed; and the three boys were again hard at work, chopping and grubbing in Mr. Lincoln's clearings. They were good-natured, jolly young fellows, and they lightened their labor with many a joke and playful prank.

Many were the droll stories with which Abraham amused his two companions. Many were the puzzling questions that he asked. Sometimes in the evening, with the other five children around him, he would declaim some piece that he had learned; or he would deliver a speech of his own on some subject of common interest.

If you could see him as he then appeared, you would hardly think that such a boy would ever become one of the most famous men of history. On his head he wore a cap made from the skin of a squirrel or a raccoon. Instead of trousers of cloth, he wore buckskin breeches, the legs of which were many inches too short. His shirt was of deerskin in the winter, and of homespun tow in the summer. Stockings he had none. His shoes were of heavy cowhide, and were worn only on Sundays or in very cold weather.

The family lived in such a way as to need very little money. Their bread was made of corn meal. Their meat was chiefly the flesh of wild game found in the forest.

Pewter plates and wooden trenchers were used on the table. The tea and coffee cups were of painted tin. There was no stove, and all the cooking was done on the hearth of the big fireplace.

But poverty was no hindrance to Abraham Lincoln. He kept on with his reading and his studies as best he could. Sometimes he would go to the little village of Gentryville, near by, to spend an evening. He would tell so many jokes and so many funny stories, that all the people would gather round him to listen.

When he was sixteen years old he went one day to Booneville, fifteen miles away, to attend a trial in court. He had never been in court before. He listened with great attention to all that was said. When the lawyer for the defense made his speech, the youth was so full of delight that he could not contain himself.

He arose from his seat, walked across the court room, and shook hands with the lawyer. "That was the best speech I ever heard," he said.

He was tall and very slim; he was dressed in a jeans coat and buckskin trousers; his feet were bare. It must have been a strange sight to see him thus complimenting an old and practiced lawyer.

From that time, one ambition seemed to fill his mind. He wanted to be a lawyer and make great speeches in court. He walked twelve miles barefooted, to borrow a copy of the laws of Indiana. Day and night he read and studied.

"Some day I shall be President of the United States," he said to some of his young friends. And this he said not as a joke, but in the firm belief that it would prove to be true.

The Boatman

One of Thomas Lincoln's friends owned a ferryboat on the Ohio River. It was nothing but a small rowboat, and would carry only three or four people at a time. This man wanted to employ some one to take care of his boat and to ferry people across the river.

Thomas Lincoln was in need of money; and so he arranged with his friend for Abraham to do this work. The wages of the young man were to be $2.50 a week. But all the money was to be his father's.

One day two strangers came to the landing. They wanted to take passage on a steamboat that was coming down the river. The ferry-boy signaled to the steamboat and it stopped in midstream. Then the boy rowed out with the two passengers, and they were taken on board.

Just as he was turning towards the shore again, each of the strangers tossed a half-dollar into his boat. He picked the silver up and looked at it. Ah, how rich he felt! He had never had so much money at one time. And he had gotten all for a few minutes' labor!

When winter came on, there were fewer people who wanted to cross the river. So, at last, the ferry-boat was tied up, and Abraham Lincoln went back to his father's home.

He was now nineteen years old. He was very tall—nearly six feet four inches in height. He was as strong as a young giant. He could jump higher and farther, and he could run faster, than any of his fellows; and there was no one, far or near, who could lay him on his back.

Although he had always lived in a community of rude, rough people, he had no bad habits. He used no tobacco; he did not drink strong liquor; no profane word ever passed his lips.

He was good-natured at all times, and kind to every one.

During that winter, Mr. Gentry, the storekeeper in the village, had bought a good deal of corn and pork. He intended, in the spring, to load this on a flatboat and send it down the river to New Orleans.

In looking about for a captain to take charge of the boat, he happened to think of Abraham Lincoln. He knew that he could trust the young man. And so a bargain was soon made. Abraham agreed to pilot the boat to New Orleans and to market the produce there; and Mr. Gentry was to pay his father eight and a half dollars a month for his services.

As soon as the ice had well melted from the river, the voyage was begun. Besides Captain Lincoln there was only one man in the crew, and that was a son of Mr. Gentry's.

The voyage was a long and weary one, but at last the two boatmen reached the great southern city. Here they saw many strange things of which they had never heard before. But they soon sold their cargo and boat, and then returned home on a steamboat.

To Abraham Lincoln the world was now very different from what it had seemed before. He longed to be away from the narrow life in the woods of Spencer county. He longed to be doing something for himself—to be making for himself a fortune and a name.

But then he remembered his mother's teachings when he sat on her knee in the old Kentucky home, "Always do right." He remembered her last words, "I know you will be kind to your father."

And so he resolved to stay with his father, to work for him, and to give him all his earnings until he was twenty-one years old.

The First Years in Illinois

Early in the spring of 1830, Thomas Lincoln sold his farm in Indiana, and the whole family moved to Illinois. The household goods were put in a wagon drawn by four yoke of oxen. The kind stepmother and her daughters rode also in the wagon.

Abraham Lincoln, with a long whip in his hand, trudged through the mud by the side of the road and guided the oxen. Who that saw him thus going into Illinois would have dreamed that he would in time become that state's greatest citizen?

The journey was a long and hard one; but in two weeks they reached Decatur, where they had decided to make their new home.

ABRAHAM LINCOLN

Abraham Lincoln was now over twenty-one years old. He was his own man. But he stayed with his father that spring. He helped him fence his land; he helped him plant his corn.

But his father had no money to give him. The young man's clothing was all worn out, and he had nothing with which to buy any more. What should he do?

Three miles from his father's cabin there lived a thrifty woman, whose name was Nancy Miller. Mrs. Miller owned a flock of sheep, and in her house there were a spinning-wheel and a loom that were always busy. And so you must know that she wove a great deal of jeans and home-made cloth.

Abraham Lincoln bargained with this woman to make him a pair of trousers. He agreed that for each yard of cloth required, he would split for her four hundred rails.

He had to split fourteen hundred rails in all; but he worked so fast that he had finished them before the trousers were ready.

The next April saw young Lincoln piloting another flatboat down the Mississippi to New Orleans. His companion this time was his mother's relative, John Hanks. This time he stayed longer in New Orleans, and he saw some things which he had barely noticed on his first trip.

He saw gangs of slaves being driven through the streets. He visited the slave-market, and saw women and girls sold to the highest bidder like so many cattle.

The young man, who would not be unkind to any living being, was shocked by these sights. "His heart bled; he was mad, thoughtful, sad, and depressed."

He said to John Hanks, "If I ever get a chance to hit that institution, I'll hit it hard, John."

He came back from New Orleans in July. Mr. Offut, the owner of the flatboat which he had taken down, then employed him to act as clerk in a country store which he had at New Salem.

New Salem was a little town not far from Springfield.

Young Lincoln was a good salesman, and all the customers liked him. Mr. Offut declared that the young man knew more than any one else in the United States, and that he could outrun and outwrestle any man in the county.

But in the spring of the next year Mr. Offut failed. The store was closed, and Abraham Lincoln was out of employment again.

The Black Hawk War

There were still a good many Indians in the West. The Sac Indians had lately sold their lands in northern Illinois to the United States. They had then moved across the Mississippi River, to other lands that had been set apart for them.

But they did not like their new home. At last they made up their minds to go back to their former hunting-grounds. They were led by a chief whose name was Black Hawk; and they began by killing the white settlers and burning their houses and crops.

This was in the spring of 1832.

The whole state of Illinois was in alarm. The governor called for volunteers to help the United States soldiers drive the Indians back.

Abraham Lincoln enlisted. His company elected him captain.

He did not know anything about military tactics. He did not know how to give orders to his men. But he did the best that he could, and learned a great deal by experience.

His company marched northward and westward until they came to the Mississippi River. But they did not meet any Indians, and so there was no fighting.

The young men under Captain Lincoln were rude fellows from the prairies and backwoods. They were rough in their manners, and hard to control. But they had very high respect for their captain.

Perhaps this was because of his great strength, and his skill in wrestling; for he could put the roughest and strongest of them on their backs. Perhaps it was because he was good-natured and kind, and, at the same time, very firm and decisive.

In a few weeks the time for which the company had enlisted came to an end. The young men were tired of being soldiers; and so all, except Captain Lincoln and one man, were glad to hurry home.

But Captain Lincoln never gave up anything half done. He enlisted again. This time he was a private in a company of mounted rangers.

The main camp of the volunteers and soldiers was on the banks of the Rock River, in northern Illinois.

Here, one day, Abraham Lincoln saw a young lieutenant of the United States army, whose name was Jefferson Davis. It is not likely that the fine young officer noticed the rough-clad ranger; but they were to know more of each other at a future time.

Three weeks after that the war was at an end. The Indians had been beaten in a battle, and Black Hawk had been taken prisoner.

But Abraham Lincoln had not been in any fight. He had not seen any Indians, except peaceable ones.

In June his company was mustered out, and he returned home to New Salem.

He was then twenty-three years old.

In the Legislature

When Abraham Lincoln came back to New Salem it was nearly time for the state election. The people of the town and neighborhood wanted to send him to the legislature, and he agreed to be a candidate.

ABRAHAM LINCOLN

It was at Pappsville, twelve miles from Springfield, that he made his first campaign speech.

He said: "Gentlemen and fellow-citizens—

"I presume you all know who I am.

"I am humble Abraham Lincoln. I have been solicited by my friends to become a candidate for the legislature.

"My politics are short and sweet.

"I am in favor of a national bank; am in favor of the internal improvement system, and a high protective tariff.

"These are my sentiments and political principles. If elected, I shall be thankful; if not, it will be all the same."

He was a tall, gawky, rough-looking fellow. He was dressed in a coarse suit of homespun, much the worse for wear.

A few days after that, he made a longer and better speech at Springfield.

But he was not elected.

About this time a worthless fellow, whose name was Berry, persuaded Mr. Lincoln to help him buy a store in New Salem. Mr. Lincoln had no money, but he gave his notes for the value of half the goods.

The venture was not a profitable one. In a few months the store was sold; but Abraham did not receive a dollar for it. It was six years before he was able to pay off the notes which he had given.

During all this time Mr. Lincoln did not give up the idea of being a lawyer. He bought a second-hand copy of *Blackstone's Commentaries* at auction. He studied it so diligently that in a few weeks he had mastered the whole of it.

He bought an old form-book, and began to draw up contracts, deeds, and all kinds of legal papers.

He would often walk to Springfield, fourteen miles away, to borrow a book; and he would master thirty or forty pages of it while returning home.

Soon he began to practice in a small way before justices of the peace and country juries. He was appointed postmaster at New Salem, but so little mail came to the place that the office was soon discontinued.

He was nearly twenty-five years old. But, with all his industry, he could hardly earn money enough to pay for his board and clothing.

He had learned a little about surveying while living in Indiana. He now took up the study again, and was soon appointed deputy surveyor of Sangamon county.

He was very skillful as a surveyor. Although his chain was only a grape-vine, he was very accurate and never made mistakes.

The next year he was again a candidate for the legislature. This time the people were ready to vote for him, and he was elected. It was no small thing for so young a man to be chosen to help make the laws of his state.

ABRAHAM LINCOLN

No man ever had fewer advantages than Abraham Lincoln. As a boy, he was the poorest of the poor. No rich friend held out a helping hand. But see what he had already accomplished by pluck, perseverance, and honesty!

He had not had access to many books, but he knew books better than most men of his age. He knew the Bible by heart; he was familiar with Shakespeare; he could repeat nearly all the poems of Burns; he knew much about physics and mechanics; he had mastered the elements of law.

He was very awkward and far from handsome, but he was so modest, so unselfish and kind, that every one who knew him liked him. He was a true gentleman—a gentleman at heart, if not in outside polish.

And so, as I have already said, Abraham Lincoln, at the age of twenty-five, was elected to the state legislature. He served the people so well that when his term closed, two years later, they sent him back for another term.

The capital of Illinois had, up to this time, been at Vandalia. Mr. Lincoln and his friends now succeeded in having a law passed to remove it to Springfield. Springfield was nearer to the center of the state; it was more convenient to everybody, and had other advantages which Vandalia did not have.

The people of Springfield were so delighted that they urged Mr. Lincoln to come there and practice law. An older lawyer, whose name was John T. Stuart, and who had a good practice, offered to take him in partnership with him.

And so, in 1837, Abraham Lincoln left New Salem and removed to Springfield. He did not have much to move. All the goods that he had in the world were a few clothes, which he carried in a pair of saddlebags, and two or three law books. He had no money, and he rode into Springfield on a borrowed horse.

He was then twenty-eight years old.

From that time on, Springfield was his home.

Politics and Marriage

The next year after his removal to Springfield, Mr. Lincoln was elected to the legislature for the third time.

There were then, in this country, two great political parties, the Democrats and the Whigs. Mr. Lincoln was a Whig, and he soon became the leader of his party in the state. But the Whigs were not so strong as the Democrats.

The legislature was in session only a few weeks each year; and so Mr. Lincoln could devote all the rest of the time to the practice of law. There were many able lawyers in Illinois; but Abe Lincoln of Springfield soon made himself known among the best of them.

In 1840, he was again elected to the legislature. This was the year in which General William H. Harrison was elected president of the United States. General

ABRAHAM LINCOLN

Harrison was a Whig; and Mr. Lincoln's name was on the Whig ticket as a candidate for presidential elector in his state.

The presidential campaign was one of the most exciting that had ever been known. It was called the "log cabin" campaign, because General Harrison had lived in a log cabin, and his opponents had sneered at his poverty.

In the East as well as in the West, the excitement was very great. In every city and town and village, wherever there was a political meeting, a log cabin was seen. On one side of the low door hung a long-handled gourd; on the other side, a coon-skin was nailed to the logs; the blue smoke curled up from the top of the stick-and-clay chimney.

You may believe that Abraham Lincoln went into this campaign with all his heart. He traveled over a part of the state, making stump-speeches for his party.

One of his ablest opponents was a young lawyer, not quite his own age, whose name was Stephen A. Douglas. In many places, during this campaign, Lincoln and Douglas met in public debate upon the questions of the day. And both of them were so shrewd, so well informed, and so eloquent, that those who heard them were unable to decide which was the greater of the two.

General Harrison was elected, but not through the help of Mr. Lincoln; for the vote of Illinois that year was for the Democratic candidate.

In 1842, when he was thirty-three years old, Mr. Lincoln was married to Miss Mary Todd, a young lady from Kentucky, who had lately come to Springfield on a visit.

For some time after their marriage, Mr. and Mrs. Lincoln lived in a hotel called the "Globe Tavern," paying four dollars a week for rooms and board. But, in 1844, Mr. Lincoln bought a small, but comfortable frame house, and in this they lived until they went to the White House, seventeen years later.

Although he had been successful as a young lawyer, Mr. Lincoln was still a poor man. But Mrs. Lincoln said: "I would rather have a good man, a man of mind, with bright prospects for success and power and fame, than marry one with all the horses and houses and gold in the world."

Congressman and Lawyer

In 1846, Mr. Lincoln was again elected to the legislature.

In the following year the people of his district chose him to be their representative in Congress. He took his seat in December. He was then thirty-nine years old. He was the only Whig from Illinois.

There were many famous men in Congress at that time. Mr. Lincoln's lifelong rival, Stephen A. Douglas, was one of the senators from Illinois. He had

ABRAHAM LINCOLN

already served a term or two in the House of Representatives.

Daniel Webster was also in the senate; and so was John C. Calhoun; and so was Jefferson Davis.

Mr. Lincoln took an active interest in all the subjects that came before Congress. He made many speeches. But, perhaps, the most important thing that he did at this time was to propose a bill for the abolition of the slave-trade in the city of Washington.

He believed that slavery was unjust to the slave and harmful to the nation. He wanted to do what he could to keep it from becoming a still greater evil. But the bill was opposed so strongly that it was not even voted upon.

After the close of Mr. Lincoln's term in Congress, he hoped that President Taylor, who was a Whig, might appoint him to a good office. But in this he was disappointed.

And so, in 1849, he returned to his home in Springfield, and again settled down to the practice of law.

He was then forty years old. Considering the poverty of his youth, he had done great things for himself. But he had not done much for his country. Outside of his own state his name was still unknown.

His life for the next few years was like that of any other successful lawyer in the newly-settled West. He had a large practice, but his fees were very small. His income from his profession was seldom more than $2,000 a year.

FOUR GREAT AMERICANS

His habits were very simple. He lived comfortably and respectably. In his modest little home there was an air of order and refinement, but no show of luxury.

No matter where he might go, Mr. Lincoln would have been known as a Western man. He was six feet four inches in height. His face was very homely, but very kind.

He was cordial and friendly in his manners. There was something about him which made everybody feel that he was a sincere, truthful, upright man. He was known among his neighbors as "Honest Abe Lincoln."

The Question of Slavery

The great subject before the country at this time was slavery. It had been the cause of trouble for many years.

In the early settlement of the American colonies, slavery had been introduced through the influence of the English government. The first slaves had been brought to Virginia nearly 240 years before the time of which I am telling you.

Many people saw from the beginning that it was an evil which would at some distant day bring disaster upon the country. In 1772, the people of Virginia petitioned the King of England to put a stop to the bringing of slaves from Africa into that colony. But the petition was rejected; and the King forbade them to speak of the matter any more.

Washington, Jefferson, and other founders of our nation looked upon slavery as an evil. They hoped that the time might come when it would be done away with; for they knew that the country would prosper better without it.

At the time of the Revolution, slavery was permitted in all the states. But it was gradually abolished, first in Pennsylvania and then in the New England states, and afterwards in New York.

In 1787, a law was passed by Congress declaring that there should be no slavery in the territory northwest of the river Ohio. This was the territory from which the states of Ohio, Indiana, Illinois, Michigan, and Wisconsin were formed; and so, of course, these states were free states from the beginning.

The great industry of the South was cotton-raising. The people of the Southern states claimed that slavery was necessary, because only negro slaves could do the work required on the big cotton plantations. Kentucky, Tennessee, Alabama, Mississippi, and Louisiana were admitted, one by one, into the Union; and all were slave states.

In 1821, Missouri applied for admission into the Union. The South wanted slavery in this state also, but the North objected. There were many hot debates in Congress over this question. At last, through the influence of Henry Clay, the dispute was settled by what has since been known as the Missouri Compromise.

The Missouri Compromise provided that Missouri should be a slave state; this was to satisfy the South. On the other hand, it declared that all the western territory north of the line which formed the southern boundary of Missouri, should forever be free; this was to appease the North.

But the cotton planters of the South grew more wealthy by the labor of their slaves. More territory was needed for the extension of slavery. Texas joined the United States and became a slave state.

Then followed a war with Mexico; and California, New Mexico and Utah were taken from that country. Should slavery be allowed in these new territories also?

At this time a new political party was formed. It was called the "Free Soil Party," and the principle for which it contended was this: *"No more slave states and no slave territory."*

This party was not very strong at first, but soon large numbers of Whigs and many northern Democrats, who did not believe in the extension of slavery, began to join it.

Although the Whig party refused to take any position against the extension of slavery, there were many anti-slavery Whigs who still remained with it and voted the Whig ticket—and one of these men was Abraham Lincoln.

The contest between freedom and slavery became more fierce every day. At last another compromise was proposed by Henry Clay.

This compromise provided that California should be admitted as a free state; that slavery should not be prohibited in New Mexico and Utah; that there should be no more markets for slaves in the District of Columbia; and that a new and very strict fugitive-slave law should be passed.

This compromise is called the "Compromise of 1850." It was in support of these measures that Daniel Webster made his last great speech.

It was hoped by Webster and Clay that the Compromise of 1850 would put an end to the agitation about slavery. "Now we shall have peace," they said. But the agitation became stronger and stronger, and peace seemed farther away than ever before.

In 1854, a bill was passed by Congress to organize the territories of Kansas and Nebraska. This bill provided that the Missouri Compromise should be repealed, and that the question of slavery in these territories should be decided by the people living in them.

The bill was passed through the influence of Stephen A. Douglas of Illinois. There was now no bar to the extension of slavery into any of the territories save that of public opinion.

The excitement all over the North was very great. In Kansas there was actual war between those who favored slavery and those who opposed it. Thinking men in all parts of the country saw that a great crisis was at hand.

ABRAHAM LINCOLN

Lincoln and Douglas

It was then that Abraham Lincoln came forward as the champion of freedom.

Stephen A. Douglas was a candidate for re-election to the Senate, and he found it necessary to defend himself before the people of his state for the part he had taken in repealing the Missouri Compromise. He went from one city to another, making speeches; and at each place Abraham Lincoln met him in joint debate.

"I do not care whether slavery is voted into or out of the territories," said Mr. Douglas. "The question of slavery is one of climate. Wherever it is to the interest of the inhabitants of a territory to have slave property, there a slave law will be enacted."

But Mr. Lincoln replied, "The men who signed the Declaration of Independence said that all men are created equal, and are endowed by their Creator with certain inalienable rights—life, liberty, and the pursuit of happiness. . . . I beseech you, do not destroy that immortal emblem of humanity, the Declaration of Independence."

At last, Mr. Douglas felt that he was beaten. He proposed that both should go home, and that there should be no more joint discussions. Mr. Lincoln agreed to this; but the words which he had spoken sank deep into the hearts of those who heard them.

The speeches of Lincoln and Douglas were printed in a book. People in all parts of the country read them. They had heard much about Stephen A. Douglas. He was called "The Little Giant." He had long been famous among the politicians of the country. It was believed that he would be the next President of the United States.

But who was this man Lincoln, who had so bravely vanquished the Little Giant? He was called "Honest Abe." There were few people outside of his state who had ever heard of him before.

Mr. Douglas returned to his seat in the United States senate. Mr. Lincoln became the acknowledged leader of the forces opposed to the extension of slavery.

In May, 1856, a convention of the people of Illinois was held in Bloomington, Illinois. It met for the purpose of forming a new political party, the chief object and aim of which should be to oppose the extension of slavery into the territories.

Mr. Lincoln made a speech to the members of this convention. It was one of the greatest speeches ever heard in this country. "Again and again, during the delivery, the audience sprang to their feet, and, by long-continued cheers, expressed how deeply the speaker had roused them."

And so the new party was organized. It was composed of the men who had formed the old Free Soil Party, together with such Whigs and Democrats as were opposed to the further growth of the slave power. But the greater number of its members were Whigs. This new party was called the Republican Party.

In June, the Republican Party held a national convention at Philadelphia, and nominated John C. Frémont for President. But the party was not strong enough to carry the election that year.

In that same month the Democrats held a convention at Cincinnati. Every effort was made to nominate Stephen A. Douglas for President. But he was beaten in his own party, on account of the action which he had taken in the repeal of the Missouri Compromise.

James Buchanan was nominated in his stead, and, in November, was elected.

And so the conflict went on.

In the year 1858 there was another series of joint debates between Lincoln and Douglas. Both were candidates for the United States senate. Their speeches were among the most remarkable ever delivered in any country.

Lincoln spoke for liberty and justice. Douglas's speeches were full of fire and patriotism. He hoped to be elected President in 1860. In the end, it was generally acknowledged that Lincoln had made the best arguments. But Douglas was reëlected to the Senate.

President of the United States

In 1860 there were four candidates for the presidency.

The great Democratic Party was divided into two branches. One branch nominated Stephen A. Douglas. The other branch, which included the larger number of the slave-owners of the South, nominated John C. Breckinridge, of Kentucky.

The remnant of the old Whig Party, now called the "Union Party," nominated John Bell, of Tennessee.

The Republican Party nominated Abraham Lincoln.

In November came the election, and a majority of all the electors chosen were for Lincoln.

The people of the cotton-growing states believed that, by this election, the Northern people intended to deprive them of their rights. They believed that the anti-slavery people intended to do much more than prevent the extension of slavery. They believed that the abolitionists were bent upon passing laws to deprive them of their slaves.

Wild rumors were circulated concerning the designs which the "Black Republicans," as they were called, had formed for their coercion and oppression. They declared that they would never submit.

ABRAHAM LINCOLN

And so, in December, the people of South Carolina met in convention, and declared that that state had seceded from the Union—that they would no longer be citizens of the United States. One by one, six other states followed; and they united to form a new government, called the Confederate States of America.

It had long been held by the men of the South that a state had the right to withdraw from the Union at any time. This was called the doctrine of States' Rights.

The Confederate States at once chose Jefferson Davis for their President, and declared themselves free and independent.

In February, Mr. Lincoln went to Washington to be inaugurated. His enemies openly boasted that he should never reach that city alive; and a plot was formed to kill him on his passage through Baltimore. But he took an earlier train than the one appointed, and arrived at the capital in safety.

On the 4th of March he was inaugurated. In his address at that time he said: "In your hands, my dissatisfied countrymen, and not in mine, is the momentous issue of civil war. Your government will not assail you. You can have no conflict without being yourselves the aggressors. You have no oath registered in heaven to destroy the government; while I shall have the most solemn one to protect and defend it."

The Confederate States demanded that the government should give up all the forts, arsenals, and public property within their limits. This, President Lincoln refused to do. He said that he could not admit that these states had withdrawn from the Union, or that they could withdraw without the consent of the people of the United States, given in a national convention.

And so, in April, the Confederate guns were turned upon Fort Sumter in Charleston harbor, and the war was begun. President Lincoln issued a call for 75,000 men to serve in the army for three months; and both parties prepared for the great contest.

It is not my purpose to give a history of that terrible war of four years. The question of slavery was now a secondary one. The men of one party were determined, at whatever hazard, to preserve the Union. The men of the other party fought to defend their doctrine of States' Rights, and to set up an independent government of their own.

President Lincoln was urged to use his power and declare all the slaves free. He answered:

"My paramount object is to save the Union, and not either to save or destroy slavery.

"If I could save the Union without freeing any slave, I would do it. If I could save it by freeing all the slaves, I would do it. If I could save it by freeing some and leaving others alone, I would also do that."

At last, however, when he saw that the success of the Union arms depended upon his freeing the slaves, he decided to do so. On the 1st of January, 1863, he issued a proclamation declaring that the slaves, in all the states or parts of states then in rebellion, should be free.

More than three millions of colored people were given their freedom.

But the war still went on. It reached a turning point, however, at the battle of Gettysburg, in July, that same year. From that time the cause of the Confederate States was on the wane. Little by little the patriots, who were struggling for the preservation of the Union, prevailed.

The End of a Great Life

At the close of Mr. Lincoln's first term, he was again elected President of the United States. The war was still going on, but the Union arms were now everywhere victorious.

His second inaugural address was very short. He did not boast of any of his achievements; he did not rejoice over the defeat of his enemies. But he said:

"With malice toward none; with charity for all; with firmness in the right, as God gives us to see the right, let us strive on to finish the work we are in; to bind up the nation's wounds; to care for him who shall have borne the battle, and for his widow and his orphan—to do all which may achieve and cherish a just and lasting peace among ourselves and with all nations."

Five weeks after that, on the 9th of April, 1865, the Confederate army surrendered, and the war was at an end.

Abraham Lincoln's work was done.

The 14th of April was Good Friday. On the evening of that day, Mr. Lincoln, with Mrs. Lincoln and two or three friends, visited Ford's Theatre in Washington.

At a few minutes past 10 o'clock, an actor whose name was John Wilkes Booth, came into the box where Mr. Lincoln sat. No one saw him enter. He pointed a pistol at the President's head, and fired. He leaped down upon the stage, shouting *"Sic semper tyrannis!* The South is avenged!" Then he ran behind the scenes and out by the stage door.

The President fell forward. His eyes closed. He neither saw, nor heard, nor felt anything that was taking place. Kind arms carried him to a private house not far away.

At twenty minutes past seven o'clock the next morning, those who watched beside him gave out the mournful news that Abraham Lincoln was dead.

He was fifty-six years old.

The whole nation wept for him. In the South as well as in the North, the people bowed themselves in grief. Heartfelt tributes of sorrow came from other lands in all parts of the world. Never, before nor since, has there been such universal mourning.

Such is the story of Abraham Lincoln. In the history of the world, there is no story more full of lessons of perseverance, of patience, of honor, of true nobility of purpose. Among the great men of all time, there has been no one more truly great than he.